WRITING DEGREE ZERO

WRITING DEGREE ZERO

ROLAND BARTHES

TRANSLATED FROM THE FRENCH BY ANNETTE LAVERS AND COLIN SMITH

 HILL AND WANG

A DIVISION OF FARRAR, STRAUS AND GIROUX

NEW YORK

Hill and Wang
A division of Farrar, Straus and Giroux
18 West 18th Street, New York 10011

Distributed in Canada by D&M Publishers, Inc.
Printed in the United States of America
Originally published in French in 1953 by Éditions du Seuil, France, as *Le Degré zéro de l'écriture*
Published in 1977 in the United States by Hill and Wang
This paperback edition, 2012

Library of Congress Control Number: 2011940622
Paperback ISBN: 978-0-374-53235-2

www.fsgbooks.com

10 9 8 7 6 5 4 3 2 1

CONTENTS

FOREWORD: NOTES ON REVOLUTION AFTER BARTHES
by Adam Thirlwell

1

In November 1952, if you were a French intellectual in Paris, you might be considering a series of questions like (1) Is It Possible to Define a Left-Wing Literature? And (2) Is This Literature Defined by Its Content? And also (3) Can a Work of Art Be Excluded from the Left by Its Form? These questions might also include (4a) Must a Left-Wing Work Necessarily Address Itself to a Mass Audience? and (4b) Is a Work That Reaches a Mass Audience Necessarily Left-Wing?

Yes, these were the questions that were being considered in Paris by its intellectuals, in a series of questions asked by the magazine *L'Observateur*. It was the era when the international stars were Bertolt Brecht and Pablo Picasso. And the Communism then shared by Picasso and Brecht was not a coincidence. The Nazi occupation had ended only eight years earlier. So Paris was still defined by networks of resistance and collaboration, presided over by Jean-Paul Sartre and Albert Camus. The world of Paris in the 1950s was a grisaille of wary politics. The philosopher Henri Lefebvre's *Critique de la vie quotidienne* had been published in 1947, and would be reissued in 1958. In it, he elaborated Marx's theory of alienation:

> As he strives to control nature and create his world, man conjures himself up a new nature. Certain of man's products function in relation to human reality like some impenetrable nature, undominated, oppressing his consciousness and will from without. Of course, this can only be an appearance; products of human activity cannot have the

same characteristics as brute, material things. And yet this appearance too is a reality: commodities, money, capital, the State, legal, economic and political institutions, ideologies—all function as though they were realities external to man.

"Genuine criticism," added Lefebvre, would therefore expose this "*unreality* in the 'reality' of the bourgeoisie . . ."

In other words, the Paris of the 1950s was intent on a meticulous engagement with the world of spectacle.

And it was in this era, in 1953, when he was thirty-eight, that Roland Barthes published his first book, *Le Degré zéro de l'écriture*. The book had grown out of his writings in left-wing journals like *L'Observateur* and in Camus's newspaper, *Combat*. Barthes would soon write for another leftist publication, the review *Théâtre populaire*, where he would introduce Brecht's plays to a French audience. He had just begun publishing the first texts that would later be collected as *Mythologies*: his small exercises in deconstructing the natural history of culture: invisible institutions like the Folies Bergères or *steak frites*. And he had recently curated in *L'Observateur* his survey of French intellectuals on the limits of literature and the left—culminating in an anxious finale: (5) Is a Left-Wing Work Destined to Have Only a Momentary Combat Value, Or, On the Contrary, Can a Left-Wing Work Last for Several Generations? As for Barthes himself, his underlying dandyism was hinted at in the short essay that accompanied these questions, which ended on a sternly unconvinced sentence: "We will know much more both about literature and about the left on the day when we will be able to explain why a writer can be of the left other than by saying it."

It was this aesthetic sternness that informed the short book he then published the following year, *Le Degré zéro de l'écriture*: his contribution to the era's nervy political obsession. Barthes's position was a melancholy skepticism. Writers wanted to be radical, both politically and formally: so okay, this was true. But the radical was always a receding dream. In the end, he wrote, toward his book's conclusion, every revolution was inauthentic, since "Revolution must of necessity borrow, from what it wants to destroy, the very image of what it wants to possess."

Barthes had already described this intuition, in exclusively literary terms, in an essay in *Combat* in 1947. There had been several political revolutions since 1789, he argued, but literature had survived them all. "No serious revolution in rhetoric," wrote Barthes, had arrived "to dissipate the imposture of a language which says it is universal, but which is only privileged." Whereas the bourgeoisie had been exposed as a particular group with a particular politics, the myth of literature as a universal had blithely continued, even though it belonged to a certain class, with access to the norms of education. And so the great question for writing nowadays, wrote Barthes, was to destabilize literature: "to separate writing from its historical—which is to say, in fact, its political—origins."

Six years later, Barthes now offered a brief, allusive, splintered description of the reasons why this might never be possible—why the politics of literature might be an enveloping trap.

In its spiked gravity, Barthes's mini-manifesto echoed other great works of the disillusioned, desperate avant-garde: like Isidore Isou's film *Traité de bave et d'éternité*, which came out in 1951, with its scratched film and asynchronous sound track; or Guy Debord's first film *Hurlements en faveur de Sade*, screened in 1952, where there are no images at all, just a white screen alternating with black. And it anticipated—a tuning fork!—the experimental decade that would follow: marked by the Algerian War, and Robbe-Grillet's new novels and theories of new novels, and Godard's movies of the 1960s, and Debord's situationist theories of spectacle, culminating in the *événements* of May 1968. For Barthes's miniature book had anticipated the basic problem: whether it was possible to be radical, in either art or politics—the twin revolutions of writing and living.

And this is kind of surprising. This little book is reckless, careless, snobbish, misinformed, underread. It is often obscure. It is always provincial. It is very much esoteric. But what would emerge in Barthes's late writing as a baroque and languid drift is already visible, in more compacted form, in *Writing Degree Zero*'s abrupt aphorisms and rakish shocks. And its persistent importance is in its deep intuition. The Paris of the 1950s was electric with a new practice: what Barthes's called, in a short review of a book by Michel Leiris, "the cultural explication of facts which are said to be natural." In other words, it was devoted to the dismantling of myths, or, in Barthes's later coinage, a massive act of *semioclasm*. And Barthes's great moment of acrobatics was to see that literature was a myth itself. Its central function, before representing the world, was to represent itself as literature. In *Writing Degree Zero*, therefore, Barthes dismantles the myth of literature. More precisely, he dismantles the myth that literature could be a revolution. And while this might seem coldly ironic, an exercise in negation, I'm not sure that this is true. Instead, I think that the deeper impulse of this book is central to all Barthes's work: an attempt to find a form of true liberation, to acknowledge the way in which we are governed by signs, and in that acknowledgement to find some kind of space in which to play. Because, on the one hand, all signification is a code, and therefore inauthentic. This is true. But in unsettling the codes, it might also be possible to reach a more profound form of meaning.

And while Barthes saw the literary problem as being nested inside the larger problem of all revolutions, I think it's possible to go further, and invert this hierarchy. The real subject of this book, or its real value for future readers, is its exposure of a central human problem: the problem of how to be new.

Its lessons, of course, were once particular to Saint-Germain—before Saint-Germain became a place of luxury spectacle. But this is no longer the era of Saint-Germain. It's the era of Kreuzberg and Belleville and Hamra. It's the era of Silver Lake.

It's the era, dear reader, of you.

2

Writing Degree Zero looks like a sequence of essays; it looks like an argument where a first part of four general essays are then given depth with a second part of six historical essays. This form, however, is a mirage. Really, the book is fractal: the assumptions of its theory run throughout its length, like a slice of *salume*. But it's true that this theory is nevertheless based on a historical outline (derived purely from French history and literature), and the sketch goes something like this: Up until the failed revolution of 1848, literature never needed to question itself, for literature and history were always on the same side. Then, with the crisis of 1848, literature lost its authority. Various factors had made this bourgeois sureness impossible: "the demographic expansion in Europe, the replacement of textile by heavy industry, that is, the birth of modern capitalism, the scission (completed by the revolution of June 1848) of French society into three mutually hostile classes, bringing the definitive ruin of liberal illusions." Until 1848, "it was bourgeois ideology itself which gave the measure of the universal by fulfilling it unchallenged." And so the bourgeois writer was happy: "sole judge of other people's woes and without anyone else to gaze on him," he wasn't "torn between his social condition and his intellectual vocation." Whereas, writes Barthes, after 1848 "this very ideology appears merely as one among many other possible others . . ." And so. "Thus is born a tragic predicament peculiar to Literature." The modes of writing begin to multiply. And each one, whether highly formalized or savagely colloquial, "sets itself up as the initial act whereby the writer acknowledges or repudiates his bourgeois condition."

At this point, after 1848, literature tried to establish itself as something that was above history—that existed in an absolute world of aesthetics. And so it had to "signify something other than its content and its individual form, something which defines its limits and imposes it as Literature." Literature, in other words, became neurotically obsessed with its own definition.

3

Yes, that is the basic historical sketch, and in the first essay, "What is Writing?," Barthes tries to define its basic terms. He invents—because he always loved to invent improvised sciences—a triad: language, style, and writing. Language is like "a Nature": it is the total horizon of a writer's native language—the entire possibility of words—while style springs from "the body and the past" of the writer. Style is solitude, opacity: it is what makes everyone's use of language irredeemably individual. But since literature is a social practice, there is also room "between a language and a style, for another formal reality: writing." *Writing*, I suppose, is what the happy student would now call *genre*. It is a pattern of linguistic and literary expectations, to be subverted or endorsed by every writer. And so the writer's choices concerning this third term are inherently political, which means that the agonies and compromises of writing prove that "there is no Literature without an Ethic of language."

In other words, after 1848, between the era of Balzac and the era of Flaubert, writers could no longer believe that their work was universal. The universal was a myth. And so, from then on, a writer's utopian desire for the universal could only be expressed in her formal choices. The particular agonies of form are an expression of literature's more general defeat. This is why Barthes could say, in his Introduction, that what he was proposing in this book was a history of the "Signs of Literature." The signs of literature would be the ways in which literature contorts itself—the moments when its very attempts to undo itself as literature prove its sadly literary condition.

And so, in the second essay, "Political Modes of Writing," Barthes derides the possibilities so far discovered of engagé writing. He returns to the idea he had sketched in his survey of French intellectuals—that a political literature could not just be the literature of people who considered themselves to be political. It had to be political in its form. And this form, so far, was impossible. In the following two essays, Barthes therefore proposed sketches of the novel and poetry. Neither offered any hope.

The novel is pure politics, while the poem is pure nature.

Barthes's chapter on the novel is one of the most gleeful and abrupt and exaggerated attacks on the novel that I can think of. The poor novel, derided as a fascist form! For the novel, argued Barthes, was written in the same falsifying mode as nineteenth-century history: they were both "plane projections of a curved and organic world." The novel was based on two conventions: the third person and the preterite (even if, of course, the social and political connotations of this tense only exist in French)—a tense that maintains a hierarchy in the realm of facts: "[T]he preterite is precisely this operative sign whereby the narrator reduces the exploded reality to a slim and pure logos, without density, without volume . . ." As opposed to the "opacity and solitude" of existence, the novelist offers a fake clarity; and so the novel as a form is inherently "reassuring" to society: the novel is conservative. The novel, in other words, is an instrument for mythologizing, a form of alienation.

And then, in the essay that follows—"Is There any Poetic Writing?"—Barthes sketches the opposite problem. Where the novel is the expression of a total orthodoxy, poetry is the expression of a desperate privacy. In poetry, "there is no mode of writing left, there are only styles, thanks to which man turns his back on society and confronts the world of objects without going through any of the forms of History or of social life." There is no such thing as poetic *writing*, according to the terms of Barthes's triad: only poetic style.

But here, I think, Barthes has reached a point of contradiction, which can be fruitful for his future reader. After all, according to the terms of Barthes's own argument, there is no way that literature can avoid the forms of history. Pure style cannot exist. Even poetry, in the end, will therefore be a form of writing, which means that even poetry will not be secluded from politics.

Yes, with this moment of contradiction, it becomes possible to imagine another answer to Barthes's paradox: a future literature.

4

But then, I'm not sure that this kind of contradiction is so important, since what's really important in Barthes's book is the basic argument—which still, I think, requires answering. It needed answering in Saint-Germain, and it now needs answering in Kreuzberg. And the argument can be summarized, perhaps, like this: Every new invention in literature figures itself as a refusal of literature, but is a refusal of literature ever possible? Is a revolution only a repetition?

And so, in Part II, Barthes tries to offer a short history of what he's been outlining: the impossibility of true literature, of literature that goes beyond its codes. There was the Flaubert experiment, which made writing into an object and a form of labor. There was the Maupassant experiment, which "set out to give the most accurate description of nature," but only produced a form of writing "loaded with the most spectacular signs of fabrication" (and I love these moments where Barthes finally offers what he had proposed: a history of the signs of literature, summarizing the conventional realist way of writing, with its metaphors "which seize the very slightest verb"—"We see that nothing here is given without metaphor, for it must be laboriously borne home to the reader that 'it is well written' (that is, that what he is consuming is Literature)." And there was the Mallarmé experiment, which tried to make literature disappear, but in the end could not—and so "this poignant self-destruction of Literature" proves only "that there is no writing which can be lastingly revolutionary, and that any silence of form can escape imposture only by complete abandonment of communication." And now, writes Barthes, in the Paris of the 1950s, there are two more experiments. There is the experiment of Camus—to create a neutral language. ("Unfortunately, nothing is more fickle than a colourless writing . . .") And there is the experiment of Céline and Queneau— "to contaminate all the parts of the written discourse by spoken speech . . ." Only Queneau's experiment, it seems, can make Barthes hopeful: "[T]he general suspicion which has gradually overtaken language throughout modern literature gives way to a reconciliation between the logos of the writer and that of men. Only then can the writer declare himself entirely committed, when his poetic freedom takes its place within a verbal condition whose limits are those of society and not those of a convention or a public."

And once again this love of Queneau—and Queneau is lovable, no question—reveals Barthes's problem. His attack on the codes of literature is so savage that no one can survive it. Even Queneau's zany style is a code like any other. But then, Barthes's manifesto was always, in a strange way, a document of tenderness. For in his conclusion, "The Utopia of Language," he states some simple stubborn truths. Every writer wants to express new content, and only has old forms to do this with. And however much a writer tries to destroy literature, however much she tries to search "for a non-style or an oral style, for a zero level or a spoken level of writing," it's impossible. And this is a literary problem, but it's also a social problem. Yes, kids: "Revolution must of necessity borrow, from what it wants to destroy, the very image of what it wants to possess." And this is why literature continues to be melancholy:

> [A]s a Necessity, it testifies to the division of languages which is inseparable from the division of classes; as Freedom, it is the consciousness of this division and the very effort which seeks to surmount it. Feeling permanently guilty of its own solitude, it is none the less an imagination eagerly desiring a felicity of words . . .

5

High-speed, furious, and also exhilarating: I keep wondering about the future of *Writing Degree Zero*. I keep wondering about its use-value. Which means that I also wonder if its use is going to be different for a reader or a writer; and whether this will differ when the reader or the writer isn't French; and whether this will differ—in the case of the writer—for a poet or a novelist, or a playwright or a film-maker. Because this text is monomaniac. And then I think: Perhaps the usefulness of *Writing Degree Zero* is precisely in this mania. So often wrong, or melodramatic, or self-righteous, it forces the reader, and the reader-writer, in any language, to examine their own myth of literature.

This book is a miniature manual.

And its value can be distributed as a zigzag across an imaginary graph. Its first permanent invention is to demonstrate that not even literature is immune from the universal process of mythmaking— that the conventions of literature are more insidious and more deep than they might first seem: in the very tenses, the actual grammar.

And while the concept of alienation might not belong to Barthes—it belongs to his friend Henri Lefebvre, via the early writings of Karl Marx—it was Barthes who applied the theory with such precision to literature. He makes it impossible for any writer to be cutely cozy: every literary choice requires its own skeptical analysis. This idea that a central effect of literature is to signal itself as literature is, I think, Barthes's crucial somersault—to have seen that literature is always verging on becoming a pure emptiness, just as later Barthes would famously argue that detail in a narrative signals not the real but the literary version of the real: detail, in the end, is just a reality effect.

And yet, and yet . . . The problem with *Writing Degree Zero* is that it leads to silence. But I'm not sure that silence is necessary. And the route toward a future literature can maybe be found if the fractious reader begins to notice how impatient Barthes is for severity. There are two forms of the avant-garde outlined in this book: the artistically avant-garde desire in a writer to write beyond a code, to destroy the old forms of literature; and the politically avant-garde desire to extend the audience for literature, to make literature a political act. And since neither will ever be realized fully, Barthes will not allow that any realization is possible at all.

I keep thinking of his description of the novel as "a Death" . . . The only solution Barthes can imagine is to linger on the threshold of literature: to write a novel that is its own atelier: in other words, the only solution is to be Proust. (Or, adds Barthes in a comically inadequate aside, perhaps a novelist can also write in the present tense.) What has disappeared here, in the elegance of his machine, is the European avant-garde. There is no Joyce, no Döblin, no Musil, no Gadda . . .

And this is a problem.

Because it's true that every writer wants to be new, even if it's also obvious that every renovation will involve a repetition. This is why Barthes's figure for the writer is Orpheus, the figure of self-cancellation—whose desire for something is so strong that it robs him of the object of his desire. But then, it's also possible to reverse the conundrum. It might never be possible to move beyond a code, since the urge to go beyond literature is a pure literary gesture. Yes, it might never be possible to write literature on the other side of literature. But the opposite is also true. It might only be possible to write literature that has a value, and a permanence, if you are desperately trying to avoid the condition of literature, just as this might be the only way to invent new forms of the political for literature. And the crazy thing is that it is Barthes himself, in his most famous aphorism from *Writing Degree Zero*, who summed this alternative up: "Literature is like phosphorus: it shines with its maximum brilliance at the moment when it attempts to die."

6

I'm a kid novelist, after all: so I still believe that the novel is a future form.

Of course the realist novel represents a code! Just as of course a narrative represents an artificial arrangement of facts! But this doesn't mean that novels can't also be truths. In his book on the historian Jules Michelet, which Barthes was writing at about the same time as *Le Degré zéro de l'écriture*, Barthes admires Michelet for his carefulness with causality: some objects of history, he writes admiringly, "are not the causes of others, they are merely the different moments of the same stem." Barthes imagined an ideal history that was an arborescence, a swarm of causes. And then I think: But this is what Gadda was examining in his novels and stories, culminating in his great unfinished novel *Quer pasticciaccio brutto de via Merulana (That Awful Mess on the Via Merulana)*, finally published four years after Barthes's essay, in 1957; just as it was what Döblin was examining in his novel *Berlin Alexanderplatz*, which had come out in 1929. In his essay "The Crisis of the Novel," also written in 1929, Walter Benjamin gorgeously described how Döblin had revised the structures of the novel:

> The stylistic principle governing this book is that of montage. Petty-bourgeois printed matter, scandalmongering,

stories of accidents, the sensational incidents of 1928, folk songs, and advertisements rain down in this text. The montage explodes the framework of the novel, bursts its limits both stylistically and structurally, and clears the way for new, epic possibilities.

Döblin's novel represented a new version of causation, of arrangement of facts—and this was because it allowed a new form of content into literature:

> The material of the montage is anything but arbitrary. Authentic montage is based on the document. In its fanatical struggle with the work of art, Dadaism used montage to turn daily life into its ally. It was the first to proclaim, somewhat uncertainly, the autocracy of the authentic. The film at its best moments made as if to accustom us to montage. Here, for the first time, it has been placed at the service of narrative.

A few years later, Benjamin would write a series of texts on Brecht (whom Barthes, after all, also admired), in which he would extend these ideas of epic and montage to the theater. Brecht's technique of montage, argued Benjamin, his systematic interruptions of the text, were his way of creating truths: "Epic theater, then, does not reproduce conditions but, rather, reveals them. This uncovering of conditions is brought about through processes being interrupted." And it's this overlap of Döblin and Benjamin and Brecht that seems to me to offer a way into a future novel that would also be true to Barthes's distrust. For this kind of montage is dedicated to the production not just of new forms but also new ways of addressing an audience. In his conclusion to the published version of his essay "What Is Epic Theater?" Benjamin wrote: "Epic theater takes account of a circumstance which has received too little attention, and which could be described as the filling-in of the orchestra pit." The stylistic innovation was also a radical politics. It couldn't help it. This doesn't mean that it represents a more general revolution. But it represents, at least, the only revolution that an art form can effect: a revolution in its means of production and consumption.

And I think of Jean-Luc Godard, who as the 1960s wore on would famously argue that it wasn't a matter of making political films, it was instead a matter of making films politically. There could be an overlap of politics and art. For the myth of literature's self-sufficiency, its absence from history, does not disprove a deeper truth: that the relation between literature and freedom is only maintained through its formal restlessness. It has nothing to do with a specific political affiliation—since, after all, a novel that proves a single political thesis is no longer a novel.

And then I think of that word *zero* in Barthes's title. It was very much a modish word. Rossellini's movie *Germania anno zero (Germany, Year Zero)* came out in 1948. Zero was the intellectuals' sign that, after World War II, everything needed to be begun again, from a position of total destitution and skepticism. Rossellini's idea of the *year zero* became Godard's signature, reused in *Made in U.S.A.*, and *2 or 3 Things I Know About Her*, and *La Chinoise*. Just as in Barthes's text, zero also represents the total new.

This is where I wonder if it's possible to hazard a future direction. Doing literature politically but artistically would involve changing the position of the reader to the work: a shift in consumption and production. Yes—this, it seems to me, is one future for the novel: its search for new forms will involve searching for new forms of addressing a reader.

But the new is complicated. And so I like the fact that the two writers Barthes would champion, in the 1950s and early 1960s, were Bertolt Brecht and Alain Robbe-Grillet. Such contradictions! Their techniques are linked only by a shared interest in destroying the myths of depth. Which shows how many possibilities remain, in the end, for a radical literature. Just as I therefore like the fact that when, in 1955, Brecht was in Paris for the French premiere of *The Caucasian Chalk Circle*, Barthes was naturally invited to meet him, but Brecht's arrival in the Latin Quarter also drew a crazed crowd of young *gauchistes*—among whom, in the crowd out on the Place Saint-Michel, was Georges Perec, trying to get a look. For in Perec's small essays into the everyday and his giant jigsaw novel *La Vie mode d'emploi*, with their mode of self-address and exhortation to the reader, yet another form of literature becomes visible. Just as it did in other agile artists, acrobatic both with their form and with the means of its production—like Godard himself, or Pasolini, or Gordon Matta-Clark; and just as had already been possible in Joyce's *Ulysses*, or in Gadda's endless stories.

In all of them, signs leave the desert of codes, and finally transform into truths.

But then, this was also what Barthes would think, in the end . . .

7

Around twenty years later, in 1975, Barthes wrote a book of autobiography that was really a book of rereading: *Roland Barthes par Roland Barthes*. In it, he offered a self-examination—a listing of his themes—describing himself as "he," his own subject: "Evidently he dreams of a world which would be exempt from meaning (as one is from military service). This began with *Writing Degree Zero*, in which is imagined 'the absence of every sign' . . ."

And he was right, I think, to note this persistent theme, which was announced in *Writing Degree Zero*. This struggle with signs as agents of power became the constant element in Barthes's work: a refusal of the falsely natural. Against the static dogma of bourgeois myth, he wanted to posit another kind of sign: the utopian, the overflowing, the excessive.

In his retrospective, he remembered how at the time of *Writing Degree Zero* the "intertext" was Sartre, Marx, and Brecht, for he was engaged in a program of "social mythology." These were the figures who might help him in his battle with signs. Gradually, however, he began to change his mind. The battle became more personal, more elliptical. He had always been in search of a mobile sign: he had always wanted, he wrote, "to side with any writing whose principle is that *the subject is merely an effect of language*." His work had been a refusal of the linguistic stereotype: "The stereotype is what *begins* to fatigue me. Whence the antidote, cited as far back as *Writing Degree Zero*: the *freshness* of language." But in his usual medium, the aphoristic essay, this freshness was always an anxiety, like his sad parenthesis: "(Doom of the essay, compared to the novel: doomed to *authenticity*—to the preclusion of quotation marks.)" There was no overflow in the essay as a form: there was no creation of infinite irony. There was, in other words, no montage.

For gradually, Barthes was coming to realize that the novel could in fact be the form he had always wanted: a form of total freedom. And so began the process of his last few years, teaching his seminars at the Collège de France, where he tried to reach a novelistic form of writing. He tried to show that a sign could—if combined in certain ways, within a structure of irony and reversal—dissolve and become the thing it represented. The reality effect was no longer the proof of a code, but a moment of truth.

This late search, of course, represents another story. But I think that it should be remembered, when reading *Writing Degree Zero*. Yes, I think that in Belleville, or Hamra, or wherever, this sudden nostalgia for the novel as a form should be trusted.

Because this is what you need to do.

You need to read this book, this strange book: *Writing Degree Zero*. You need to be defeated by it. And then you need (like Barthes) to begin a revolution.

NOTES

vii "As he strives to control nature": Henri Lefebvre, *Critique of Everyday Life*, Volume 1 (London: Verso, 1991), p. 169.

viii "Genuine criticism": Ibid., p. 168.

viii "We will know much more": Roland Barthes, *Oeuvres Complètes*, Volume 1, ed. Eric Marty (Paris: Seuil, 2002), p. 165.

ix "Revolution must of necessity borrow": Roland Barthes, *Writing Degree Zero* (New York: Hill and Wang, 2012), p. 87.

ix "No serious revolution in rhetoric": Barthes, *Oeuvres Complètes*, Volume 1, p. 97.

ix "to separate writing": Ibid., p. 97.

x "the cultural explication of facts": Ibid., p. 128.

xi "the demographic expansion in Europe": Barthes, *Writing Degree Zero*, p. 60.

xi   "it was bourgeois ideology itself": Ibid., p. 60.

xi   "sole judge of other": Ibid., p. 60.

xi   "torn between his": Ibid., p. 60.

xi   "this very ideology appears": Ibid., p. 60.

xi   "Thus is born a tragic predicament": Ibid., p. 86.

xi   "sets itself up as the initial act": Ibid., pp. 60–61.

xi   "signify something other": Ibid., pp. 1–2.

xi   "a Nature": Ibid., p. 13.

xii   "the body and the past": Ibid., p. 10.

xii   "between a language": Ibid., p. 13.

xii   "there is no Literature": Ibid., p. 6.

xii   "Signs of Literature": Ibid., p. 2.

xii   "plane projections": Ibid., p. 29.

xiii   "[T]he preterite is precisely": Ibid., p. 30.

xiii   "opacity and solitude": Ibid., p. 31.

xiii   "reassuring": Ibid., p. 32.

xiii   "there is no mode of writing left": Ibid., p. 52.

xiv   "set out to give the most accurate description": Ibid., p. 67.

xiv   "loaded with the most spectacular signs": Ibid., p. 68.

xiv   "which seize the very slightest verb": Ibid., p. 71.

xiv   "We see that nothing here": Ibid., p. 71.

xiv   "this poignant self-destruction": Ibid., p. 75.

xiv   "that there is no writing": Ibid., p. 75.

xiv   "Unfortunately, nothing": Ibid., p. 78.

xiv   "to contaminate all the parts": Ibid., p. 82.

xiv   "[T]he general suspicion": Ibid., p. 83.

xv   "for a non-style or an oral style": Ibid., p. 87.

xv   "Revolution must": Ibid., p. 87.

xv   "[A]s a Necessity": Ibid., p. 87.

xvi   "a Death": Ibid., p. 39.

xvii   "Literature is like phosphorus": Ibid., p. 38.

xvii   "are not the causes": Roland Barthes, *Michelet* (New York: Hill and Wang, 1987), p. 35.

xvii   "The stylistic principle": Walter Benjamin, "The Crisis of the Novel," in *Selected Writings*, Volume 2 (Cambridge: Harvard University Press, 1999), p. 301.

xviii   "The material of the montage": Ibid., p. 301.

xviii   "What Is Epic Theater?": Walter Benjamin, "What Is Epic Theater?," in *Understanding Brecht* (London: Verso, 1998), pp. 4–5.

xviii   "Epic theater takes account": Ibid., p. 22.

xx   "Evidently he dreams": Roland Barthes, *Roland Barthes by Roland Barthes* (New York: Hill and Wang, 2010), p. 87.

xx   "intertext": Ibid., p. 145.

xx   "social mythology": Ibid., p. 145.

xx   "to side with any writing": Ibid., p. 79.

xxi   "The stereotype is what *begins*": Ibid., p. 89.

xxi   "(Doom of the essay": Ibid., p. 89.

INTRODUCTION

Hébert, the revolutionary, never began a number of his news-sheet *Le Père Duchêne* without introducing a sprinkling of obscenities. These improprieties had no real meaning, but they had significance. In what way? In that they expressed a whole revolutionary situation. Now here is an example of a mode of writing* whose function is no longer only communication or expression, but the imposition of something beyond language, which is both History and the stand we take in it.

It is impossible to write without labelling oneself: as with *Le Père Duchêne*, so equally with Literature. It too must signify something other than its content and its individual form, something which defines its

* *Ecriture*, which in French normally means only 'handwriting' or 'the art of writing', is now more and more frequently used as a substantive corresponding to all senses of the verb *écrire*, generally to mean the style, the fact of composing a work, or the actions which properly belong to a writer. It is used here in a strictly technical sense to denote a new concept, and is translated as 'writing', 'mode of writing'. This concept is discussed further in relation to that of 'idiolect' in *Elements of Semiology* (I.1.6 and I.1.7), as is that of 'zero degree'.

limits and imposes it as Literature. Whence a set of
signs unrelated to the ideas, the language or the style,
and setting out to give definition, within the body of
every possible mode of expression, to the utter
separateness of a ritual language. This hieratic quality
of written Signs establishes Literature as an institution and clearly tends to place it above History, for
no limits can be set without some idea of permanence. Now it is when History is denied that it is
most unmistakably at work; it is therefore possible to
trace a history of literary expression which is neither
that of a particular language, nor that of the various
styles, but simply that of the Signs of Literature, and
we can expect that this purely formal history may
manifest, in its far from obscure way, a link with the
deeper levels of History.

We are naturally concerned with a link the form
of which may well vary with History itself; there is
no need to invoke direct determinism in order to feel
that History underlies the fortunes of modes of writing: this kind of functional front, which sweeps
along events, situations and ideas in the current of
historical time, does not so much produce effects as
set limits to choice. History, then, confronts the
writer with a necessary option between several moral
attitudes connected with language; it forces him to
signify Literature in terms of possibilities outside his
control. We shall see, for example, that the ideo-
logical unity of the bourgeoisie gave rise to a single

mode of writing, and that in the bourgeois periods (classical and romantic), literary form could not be divided because consciousness was not; whereas, as soon as the writer ceased to be a witness to the universal, to become the incarnation of a tragic awareness (around 1850), his first gesture was to choose the commitment of his form, either by adopting or rejecting the writing of his past. Classical writing therefore disintegrated, and the whole of Literature, from Flaubert to the present day, became the problematics of language.

This was precisely the time when Literature (the word having come into being shortly before) was finally established as an object. Classical art could have no sense of being a language, for it *was* language, in other words it was transparent, it flowed and left no deposit, it brought ideally together a universal Spirit and a decorative sign without substance or responsibility; it was a language 'closed' by social and not natural bounds. It is a well-known fact that towards the end of the eighteenth century this transparency becomes clouded; literary form develops a second-order power independent of its economy and euphemistic charm; it fascinates the reader, it strikes him as exotic, it enthralls him, it acquires a weight. Literature is no longer felt as a socially privileged mode of transaction, but as a language having body and hidden depths, existing both as dream and menace.

This is important: literary form may henceforth elicit those existential feelings lying at the heart of any object: a sense of strangeness or familiarity, disgust or indulgence, utility or murder. For a century now, every mode of writing has thus been an exercise in reconciliation with, or aversion from, that objectified Form inevitably met by the writer on his way, and which he must scrutinize, challenge and accept with all its consequences, since he cannot ever destroy it without destroying himself as a writer. Form hovers before his gaze like an object; whatever he does, it is a scandal: if it stands resplendent, it appears outmoded; if it is a law unto itself, it is asocial; in so far as it is particular in relation to time or mankind, it cannot but mean solitude.

The whole nineteenth century witnessed the progress of this dramatic phenomenon of concretion. In Chateaubriand it is still only a trace, a light pressure of linguistic euphoria, a kind of narcissism in which the manner of writing is scarcely separable from its instrumental function and merely mirrors itself. Flaubert – to take only the typical stages of this process – finally established Literature as an object, through promoting literary labour to the status of a value; form became the end-product of craftsmanship, like a piece of pottery or a jewel (one must understand that craftsmanship was here made manifest, that is, it was for the first time imposed on the reader as a spectacle). Mallarmé's work, finally, was the crowning achievement of this creation of Literature as Object, and this by the ultimate of all objectifying acts: murder. For we know that the whole effort of Mallarmé was exerted towards the destruction of language, with Literature reduced, so to speak, to being its carcass.

From an initial non-existence in which thought, by a happy miracle, seemed to stand out against the backcloth of words, writing thus passed through all the stages of a progressive solidification; it was first the object of a gaze, then of creative action, finally of murder, and has reached in our time a last metamorphosis, absence: in those neutral modes of writing, called here 'the zero degree of writing', we can easily discern a negative momentum, and an inability to maintain it within time's flow, as if Literature, having tended for a hundred years now to transmute its surface into a form with no antecedents, could no longer find purity anywhere but in the absence of all signs, finally proposing the realization of this Orphean dream: a writer without Literature. Colourless writing like Camus's, Blanchot's or Cayrol's, for example, or conversational writing like Queneau's, represents the last episode of a Passion of writing, which recounts stage by stage the disintegration of bourgeois consciousness.

What we hope to do here is to sketch this connection; to affirm the existence of a formal reality independent of language and style; to try to show that this third dimension of Form equally, and not without an additional tragic implication, binds the writer to his society; finally to convey the fact that there is no Literature without an Ethic of language. The limited length of this essay (a few pages of which appeared in 1947 and 1950 in *Combat*) is sufficient indication that what is offered here is no more than an Introduction to what a History of Writing might be.

Part One

WHAT IS WRITING?

We know that a language is a corpus of pre-scriptions and habits common to all the writers of a period. Which means that a language is a kind of natural ambience wholly pervading the writer's expression, yet without endowing it with form or content: it is, as it were, an abstract circle of truths, outside of which alone the solid residue of an individual *logos* begins to settle. It enfolds the whole of literary creation much as the earth, the sky and the line where they meet outline a familiar habitat for mankind. It is not so much a stock of materials as a horizon, which implies both a boundary and a perspective; in short, it is the comforting area of an ordered space. The writer literally takes nothing from it; a language is for him rather a frontier, to overstep which alone might lead to the linguistically supernatural; it is a field of action, the definition of, and hope for, a possibility. It is not the locus of a social commitment, but merely a reflex response involving no choice, the undivided property of men, not of writers; it remains outside the ritual of Letters; it is a social object by definition, not by option. No one can without formalities pretend to insert his freedom as a writer into the resistant medium of language because, behind the latter, the whole of History stands unified and complete in the manner of a Natural Order. Hence, for the writer, a language is nothing but a human horizon which provides a distant setting of *familiarity*, the value of which, incidentally, is entirely negative: to say that Camus and Queneau speak the same language is merely to presume, by a differential operation, all languages, archaic and futuristic, that they do not use. Suspended between forms either disused or as yet unknown, the writer's language is not so much a fund to be drawn on as an extreme limit; it is the geometrical *locus* of all that he could not say without, like Orpheus looking back, losing the stable meaning of his enterprise and his essential gesture as a social being.

A language is therefore on the hither side of Literature. Style is almost beyond it: imagery, delivery, vocabulary spring from the body and the past of the writer and gradually become the very reflexes of his art. Thus under the name of style a self-sufficient language is evolved which has its roots only in the depths of the author's personal and secret mythology, that subnature of expression where the first coition of words and things takes place, where once and for all the great verbal themes of his existence come to be installed. Whatever its sophistication, style has always something crude about it: it is a form with no clear destination, the product of a thrust, not an intention, and, as it were, a vertical and lonely dimension of thought. Its frame of reference is biological or biographical, not historical: it is the writer's 'thing', his glory and his prison, it is his solitude. Indifferent to society and transparent to it, a closed personal process, it is in no way the product of a choice or of a reflection on Literature. It is the private portion of the ritual, it rises up from the writer's myth-laden depths and unfolds beyond his area of control. It is the decorative voice of hidden, secret flesh; it works as does Necessity, as if, in this kind of floral growth, style were no more than the outcome of a blind and stubborn metamorphosis starting from a sub-language elaborated where flesh and external reality come together. Style is properly speaking a germinative phenomenon, the transmutation of a Humour. Hence stylistic overtones are distributed in depth; whereas speech has a horizontal structure, its secrets are on a level with the words in which they are couched, and what it conceals is revealed by the very duration of its flow. In speech, everything is held forth, meant for immediate consumption, and words, silences and their common mobility are launched towards a meaning superseded: it is a transfer leaving no trace and brooking no delay. Style, on the other hand, has only a vertical dimension, it plunges into the closed recollection of the person and achieves its opacity from a certain experience of matter; style is never anything but metaphor, that is, equivalence of the author's literary intention and carnal structure (it must be remembered that structure is the residual deposit of duration). So that style is always a secret; but the occult aspect of its implications does not arise from the mobile and ever-provisional nature of language; its secret is recollection locked within the body of the writer. The allusive virtue of style is not a matter of speed, as in speech, where what is unsaid nevertheless remains as an interim of language, but a matter of density, for what stands firmly and deeply beneath style, brought together harshly or tenderly in its figures of speech, are fragments of a reality entirely alien to language. The miracle of this transmutation makes style a kind of supra-literary operation which carries man to the threshold of power and magic. By reason of its biological origin, style resides outside art, that is, outside the pact which binds the writer to society. Authors may therefore be imagined who prefer the security of art to the loneliness of style. The very type of an author without a style is Gide, whose craftsmanlike approach exploits the pleasure the moderns derive from a certain classical ethos, just as Saint-Saëns has composed in Bach's idiom, or Poulenc in Schubert's. In contrast, modern poetry – such as Hugo's, Rimbaud's or Char's – is saturated with style and is *art* only by virtue of an intention to be Poetry. It is the Authority of style, that is, the entirely free relationship between language and its fleshly double, which places the writer above History as the freshness of Innocence.

A language is therefore a horizon, and style a vertical dimension, which together map out for the writer a Nature, since he does not choose either. The language functions negatively, as the initial limit of the possible, style is a Necessity which binds the writer's humour to his form of expression. In the former, he finds a familiar History, in the latter, a familiar personal past. In both cases he deals with a Nature, that is, a familiar repertory of gestures, a gestuary, as it were, in which the energy expended is purely operative, serving here to enumerate, there to transform, but never to appraise or signify a choice.

Now every Form is also a Value, which is why there is room, between a language and a style, for another formal reality: writing. Within any literary form, there is a general choice of tone, of ethos, if you like, and this is precisely where the writer shows himself clearly as an individual because this is where he commits himself. A language and a style are data prior to all problematics of language, they are the natural product of Time and of the person as a biological entity; but the formal identity of the writer is truly established only outside the permanence of grammatical norms and stylistic constants, where the written continuum, first collected and enclosed within a perfectly innocent linguistic nature, at last becomes a total sign, the choice of a human attitude, the affirmation of a certain Good. It thus commits the writer to manifest and communicate a state of happiness or malaise, and links the form of his utterance, which is at once normal and singular, to the vast History of the Others. A language and a style are blind forces; a mode of writing is an act of historical solidarity. A language and a style are objects; a mode of writing is a function: it is the relationship between creation and society, the literary language transformed by its social finality, form considered as a human intention and thus linked to the great crises of History. Mérimée and Fénelon, for instance, are separated by linguistic phenomena and contingent features of style; yet they make use of a language charged with the same intentionality, their ideas of form and content share a common framework, they accept the same type of conventions, the same technical reflexes work through both of them. Although separated by a century and a half, they use exactly the same instrument in the same way: an instrument perhaps a little changed in outward appearance, but not at all in the place and manner of its employment. In short, they have the same mode of writing. In contrast, writers who are almost contemporaries, Mérimée and Lautréamont, Mallarmé and Céline, Gide

and Queneau, Claudel and Camus, who have shared
or who share our language at the same stage of its
historical development use utterly different modes of
writing. Everything separates them: tone, delivery,
purpose, ethos, and naturalness of expression: the
conclusion is that to live at the same time and share
the same language is a small matter compared with
modes of writing so dissimilar and so sharply defined
by their very dissimilarity.

These modes of writing, though different, are com-
parable, because they owe their existence to one
identical process, namely the writer's consideration
of the social use which he has chosen for his form,
and his commitment to this choice. Placed at the
centre of the problematics of literature, which cannot
exist prior to it, writing is thus essentially the moral-
ity of form, the choice of that social area within
which the writer elects to situate the Nature of his
language. But this social area is by no means that of
an actual consumption. It is not a question for the
writer of choosing the social group for which he is to
write: well he knows that, save for the possibility of
a Revolution, it can only be for the self same society.
His choice is a matter of conscience, not of efficacy.
His writing is a way of conceiving Literature, not of
extending its limits. Or better still: it is because the
writer cannot modify in any way the objective data
which govern the consumption of literature (these
purely historical data are beyond his control even if

he is aware of them), that he voluntarily places the need for a free language at the sources of this language and not in its eventual consumption. So that writing is an ambiguous reality : on the one hand, it unquestionably arises from a confrontation of the writer with the society of his time; on the other hand, from this social finality, it refers the writer back, by a sort of tragic reversal, to the sources, that is to say, the instruments of creation. Failing the power to supply him with a freely consumed language, History suggests to him the demand for one freely produced.

Thus the choice of, and afterwards the responsibility for, a mode of writing point to the presence of Freedom, but this Freedom has not the same limits at different moments of History. It is not granted to the writer to choose his mode of writing from a kind of non-temporal store of literary forms. It is under the pressure of History and Tradition that the possible modes of writing for a given writer are established; there is a History of Writing. But this History is dual : at the very moment when general History proposes – or imposes – new problematics of the literary language, writing still remains full of the recollection of previous usage, for language is never innocent : words have a second-order memory which mysteriously persists in the midst of new meanings. Writing is precisely this compromise between freedom and remembrance, it is this freedom which remembers and is free only in the gesture of choice, but is no longer so within duration. True, I can today select such and such mode of writing, and in so doing assert my freedom, aspire to the freshness of novelty or to a tradition; but it is impossible to develop it within duration without gradually becoming a prisoner of someone else's words and even of my own. A stubborn after-image, which comes from all the previous modes of writing and even from the past of my own, drowns the sound of my present words. Any written trace precipitates, as inside a chemical at first transparent, innocent and neutral, mere duration gradually reveals in suspension a whole past of increasing density, like a cryptogram.

Writing as Freedom is therefore a mere moment. But this moment is one of the most explicit in History, since History is always and above all a choice and the limits of this choice. It is because writing derives from a meaningful gesture of the writer that it reaches the deeper layers of History, much more palpably than does any other cross-section of literature. The unity of classical writing, which remained uniform for centuries, the plurality of its modes in modern times, increased in the last hundred years until it came near to questioning the very fact of literature, this kind of disintegration of French writing does indeed correspond to a great crisis in general History, which is noticeable in literary History proper, only much more confusedly. What separates the 'thought' of a Balzac from that of a Flaubert is a variation within the same school; what contrasts their modes of writing is an essential break, at the precise moment when a new economic structure is joined on to an older one, thereby bringing about decisive changes in mentality and consciousness.

POLITICAL MODES OF WRITING

All modes of writing have in common the fact of being 'closed' and thus different from spoken language. Writing is in no way an instrument for communication, it is not an open route through which there passes only the intention to speak. A whole disorder flows through speech and gives it this self-devouring momentum which keeps it in a perpetually suspended state. Conversely, writing is a hardened language which is self-contained and is in no way meant to deliver to its own duration a mobile series of approximations. It is on the contrary meant to impose, thanks to the shadow cast by its system of signs, the image of a speech which had a structure even before it came into existence. What makes writing the opposite of speech is that the former always *appears* symbolical, introverted, ostensibly turned towards an occult side of language, whereas the second is nothing but a flow of empty signs, the movement of which alone is significant. The whole of speech is epitomized in this expendability of words, in this froth ceaselessly swept onwards, and speech is found only where language self-evidently functions like a devouring process which swallows only the moving crest of the words. Writing, on the contrary, is always rooted in something beyond language, it develops like a seed, not like a line, it manifests an essence and holds the threat of a secret, it is an anti-communication, it is intimidating. All writing will therefore contain the ambiguity of an object which is both language and coercion: there exists fundamentally in writing a 'circumstance' foreign to language, there is, as it were, the weight of a gaze conveying an intention which is no longer linguistic. This gaze may well express a passion of language, as in literary modes of writing; it may also express the threat of retribution, as in political ones: writing is then meant to unite at a single stroke the reality of the acts and the ideality of the ends. This is why power, or the shadow cast by power, always ends in creating an axiological writing, in which the distance which usually separates fact from value disappears within the very space of the word, which is given at once as description and as judgment. The word becomes an alibi, that is, an elsewhere and a justification. This, which is true of the literary modes of writing, in which the unity of the signs is ceaselessly fascinated by zones of infra- or ultra-language, is even truer of the political ones, in which the alibi stemming from language is at the same time intimidation and glorification: for it is power or conflict which produce the purest types of writing.

We shall see later that classical writing was a ceremonial which manifested the implantation of the writer into a particular political society, and that to speak like Vaugelas meant in the first place to be connected with the exercise of power. The Revolution did not modify the norms of this writing, since its force of thinkers remained, all things considered, the same, having merely passed from intellectual to political power; but the exceptional conditions of the struggle nevertheless brought about, within the great Form of classicism, a revolutionary mode of writing proper, defined not by its structure (which was more conventional than ever) but by its closed character and by its counterpart, since the use of language was then linked, as never before in history, to the Blood which had been shed. The Revolutionaries had no reason to wish to alter classical writing; they were in no way aware of questioning the nature of man, still less his language, and an 'instrument' they had inherited from Voltaire, Rousseau or Vauvenargues could not appear to them as compromised. It was the singularity of the historical circumstances which produced the identity of the revolutionary mode of writing. Baudelaire spoke somewhere of the 'grandiloquent truth of gestures on life's great occasions'. The Revolution was in the highest degree one of those great occasions when truth, through the bloodshed that it costs, becomes so weighty that its expression demands the very forms of theatrical amplification.

Revolutionary writing was the one and only grand
gesture commensurate with the daily presence of the
guillotine. What today appears turgid was then no
more than life-size. This writing, which bears all the
signs of inflation, was an exact writing: never was
language more incredible, yet never was it less spurious. This grandiloquence was not only form modelled
on drama; it was also the awareness of it. Without
this extravagant pose, typical of all the great revolutionaries, which enabled Guadet, the Girondin, when
arrested at Saint-Emilion, to declare without looking
ridiculous, since he was about to die: 'Yes, I am
Guadet. Executioner, do your duty. Go take my head
to the tyrants of my country. It has always turned
them pale; once severed, it will turn them paler still',
the Revolution could not have been this mythical
event which made History fruitful, along with all
future ideas on revolution. Revolutionary writing was
so to speak the entelechy of the revolutionary
legend: it struck fear into men's hearts and imposed
upon them a citizen's sacrament of Bloodshed.

Marxist writing is of a different order. Here the
closed character of the form does not derive from
rhetorical amplification or from grandiloquence in
delivery, but from a lexicon as specialized and as
functional as a technical vocabulary; even metaphors

are here severely codified. French revolutionary writing always proclaimed a right founded on bloodshed or moral justification, whereas from the very start Marxist writing is presented as the language of knowledge. Here, writing is univocal, because it is meant to maintain the cohesion of a Nature; it is the lexical identity of this writing which allows it to impose a stability in its explanations and a permanence in its method; it is only in the light of its whole linguistic system that Marxism is perceived in all its political implications. Marxist writing is as much given to understatement as revolutionary writing is to grandiloquence, since each word is no longer anything but a narrow reference to the set of principles which tacitly underlie it. For instance, the word 'imply', frequently encountered in Marxist writing, does not there have its neutral dictionary meaning: it always refers to a precise historical process, and is like an algebraical sign representing a whole bracketed set of previous postulates.

Being linked to action, Marxist writing has rapidly become, in fact, a language expressing value-judgments. This character, already visible in Marx, whose writing however remains in general explanatory, has come to pervade writing completely in the era of triumphant Stalinism. Certain outwardly similar notions, for which a neutral vocabulary would not seek a dual designation, are evaluatively parted from each other, so that each element gravitates towards a

23

different noun: for instance, 'cosmopolitanism' is the negative of 'internationalism' (already in Marx). In the Stalinist world, in which *definition*, that is to say the separation between Good and Evil, becomes the sole content of all language, there are no more words without values attached to them, so that finally the function of writing is to cut out one stage of a process: there is no more lapse of time between naming and judging, and the closed character of language is perfected, since in the last analysis it is a value which is given as explanation of another value. For instance, it may be alleged that such and such a criminal has engaged in activities harmful to the interests of the state; which boils down to saying that a criminal is someone who commits a crime. We see that this is in fact a tautology, a device constantly used in Stalinist writing. For the latter no longer aims at founding a Marxist version of the facts, or a revolutionary rationale of actions, but at presenting reality in a prejudged form, thus imposing a reading which involves immediate condemnation: the objective content of the word 'deviationist' puts it into a penological category. If two deviationists band together, they become 'fractionists', which does not involve an objectively different crime, but an increase in the sentence imposed. One can enumerate a properly Marxist writing (that of Marx and Lenin) and a writing of triumphant Stalinism; there certainly is as well a Trotskyist writing and a tactical writing, for instance that of the French Communist party with its substitution of 'people', then of 'plain folk', for 'working class', and the wilful ambiguity of terms like 'democracy', 'freedom', 'peace', etc.

There is no doubt at all that each regime has its own writing, no history of which has yet been written. Since writing is the spectacular commitment of language, it contains at one and the same time, thanks to a valuable ambiguity, the reality and the appearance of power, what it is, and what it would like to be thought to be: a history of political modes of writing would therefore be the best of social phenomenologies. For instance, the French Restoration evolved a class writing by means of which repression was immediately given as a condemnation spontaneously arising from classical 'Nature': workers claiming rights were always 'trouble-makers', strike-breakers were 'good workmen', and the subservience of judges became, in this language, the 'paternal vigilance of magistrates' (it is thanks to a similar procedure that Gaullism today calls Communists 'separatists'). We see that here the function of writing is to maintain a clear conscience and that its mission is fraudulently to identify the original fact with its remotest subsequent transformation by bolstering up the justification of actions with the additional guarantee of its own reality. This fact about writing is, by the way, typical of all authoritarian regimes; it is what might be called police-state writing: we know, for example, that the content of the word 'Order' always indicates repression.

The spreading influence of political and social facts into the literary field of consciousness has produced a new type of scriptor, halfway between the party member and the writer, deriving from the former an ideal image of committed man, and from the latter the notion that a written work is an act. Thus while the intellectual supersedes the writer, there appears in periodicals and in essays a militant mode of writing entirely freed from stylistic considerations, and which is, so to speak, a professional language signifying 'presence'. In this mode of writing, nuances abound. Nobody will deny that there is such a thing, for instance, as a writing typical of *Esprit* or of *Les Temps Modernes*.* What these intellectual modes of writing have in common, is that in them language, instead of being a privileged area, tends to become the sufficient sign of commitment. To come to adopt a closed sphere of language under the pressure of all those who do not speak it, is to proclaim one's act of choosing, if not necessarily one's agreement with that choice. Writing here resembles the signature one

* *Esprit* and *Les Temps Modernes* are two prominent monthlies, the first Left-wing Catholic and the second directed by J.-P. Sartre.

affixes at the foot of a collective proclamation one has not written oneself. So that to adopt a mode of writing – or, even better, to make it one's own – means to save oneself all the preliminaries of a choice, and to make it quite clear that one takes for granted the reasons for such a choice. Any intellectual writing is therefore the first of the 'leaps of the intellect'. Whereas an ideally free language never could function as a sign of my own person and would give no information whatsoever about my history and my freedom, the writing to which I entrust myself already exists entirely as an institution; it reveals my past and my choice, it gives me a history, it blazons forth my situation, it commits me without my having to declare the fact. Form thus becomes more than ever an autonomous object, meant to signify a property which is collective and protected, and this object is a trouble-saving device: it functions as an economy signal whereby the scriptor constantly imposes his conversion without ever revealing how it came about.

This duplicity of today's intellectual modes of writing is emphasized by the fact that in spite of the efforts made in our time, it has proved impossible successfully to liquidate Literature entirely: it still constitutes a verbal horizon commanding respect. The intellectual is still only an incompletely transformed writer, and unless he scuttles himself and becomes for ever a militant who no longer writes (some have done so, and are therefore forgotten), he cannot but come back to the fascination of former modes of writing, transmitted through Literature as an instrument intact but obsolete. These intellectual modes of writing are therefore unstable, they remain literary to the extent that they are powerless, and are political only through their obsession with commitment. In short, we are still dealing with ethical modes of writing, in which the conscience of the scriptor (one no longer ventures to call him a writer) finds the comforting image of collective salvation.

But just as, in the present state of History, any political mode of writing can only uphold a police world, so any intellectual mode of writing can only give rise to a para-literature, which no longer dares to speak its name. Both are therefore in a complete blind alley, they can lead only to complicity or impotence, which means, in either case, to alienation.

WRITING AND THE NOVEL

The Novel and History have been closely related in the very century which witnessed their greatest development. Their link in depth, that which should allow us to understand at once Balzac and Michelet, is that in both we find the construction of an autarkic world which elaborates its own dimensions and limits, and organizes within these its own Time, its own Space, its population, its own set of objects and its myths.

This sphericity of the great works of the nineteenth century found its expression in those long recitatives, the Novel and History, which are, as it were, plane projections of a curved and organic world of which the serial story which came into being at that precise moment, presents, through its involved complications, a degraded image. And yet narration is not necessarily a law of the form. A whole period could conceive novels in letters, for instance; and another can evolve a practice of History by means of analyses. Therefore Narration, as a form common to both the Novel and to History, does remain, in general, the choice or the expression of an historical moment.

Obsolete in spoken French, the preterite, which is the cornerstone of Narration, always signifies the presence of Art; it is a part of a ritual of Letters. Its function is no longer that of a tense. The part it plays is to reduce reality to a point of time, and to abstract, from the depth of a multiplicity of experiences, a pure verbal act, freed from the existential roots of knowledge, and directed towards a logical link with other acts, other processes, a general movement of the world: it aims at maintaining a hierarchy in the realm of facts. Through the preterite, the verb implicitly belongs with a causal chain, it partakes of a set of related and orientated actions, it functions as the algebraic sign of an intention. Allowing as it does an ambiguity between temporality and causality, it calls for a sequence of events, that is, for an intelligible Narrative. This is why it is the ideal instrument for every construction of a world; it is the unreal time of cosmogonies, myths, History and Novels. It presupposes a world which is constructed, elaborated, self-sufficient, reduced to significant lines, and not one which has been sent sprawling before us, for us to take or leave. Behind the preterite there always lurks a demiurge, a God or a reciter. The world is not unexplained since it is told like a story; each one of its accidents is but a circumstance, and the preterite is precisely this operative sign whereby the narrator reduces the exploded reality to a slim and pure logos, without density, without volume, without spread, and whose sole function is to unite as rapidly as possible a cause and an end. When the historian states that the duc de Guise died on December 23rd, 1588, or when the novelist relates that the Marchioness went out at five o'clock,* such actions emerge from a past without substance; purged of the uncertainty of existence, they have the stability and outline of an algebra, they are a recollection, but a useful recollection, the interest of which far surpasses its duration.

So that finally the preterite is the expression of an order, and consequently of a euphoria. Thanks to it, reality is neither mysterious nor absurd; it is clear, almost familiar, repeatedly gathered up and contained in the hand of a creator; it is subjected to the ingenious pressure of his freedom. For all the great storytellers of the nineteenth century, the world may be full of pathos but it is not derelict, since it is a grouping of coherent relations, since there is no overlapping between the written facts, since he who tells the story has the power to do away with the opacity and the solitude of the existences which made it up, since he can in all sentences bear witness to a communication and a hierarchy of actions and since, to tell the truth, these very actions can be reduced to mere signs.

* The sentence which for Valéry epitomized the conventions of the novel.

The narrative past is therefore a part of a security system for Belles-Lettres. Being the image of an order, it is one of those numerous formal pacts made between the writer and society for the justification of the former and the serenity of the latter. The preterite *signifies* a creation: that is, it proclaims and imposes it. Even from the depth of the most sombre realism, it has a reassuring effect because, thanks to it, the verb expresses a closed, well-defined, substantival act, the Novel has a name, it escapes the terror of an expression without laws: reality becomes slighter and more familiar, it fits within a style, it does not outrun language. Literature remains the currency in use in a society apprised, by the very form of words, of the meaning of what it consumes. On the contrary, when the Narrative is rejected in favour of other literary genres, or when, within the narration, the preterite is replaced by less ornamental forms, fresher, more full-blooded and nearer to speech (the present tense or the present perfect), Literature becomes the receptacle of existence in all its density and no longer of its meaning alone. The acts it recounts are still separated from History, but no longer from people.

We now understand what is profitable and what is intolerable in the preterite as used in the Novel: it is a lie made manifest, it delineates an area of plausibility which reveals the possible in the very act of unmasking it as false. The teleology common to the

Novel and to narrated History is the alienation of the facts: the preterite is the very act by which society affirms its possession of its past and its possibility. It creates a content credible, yet flaunted as an illusion; it is the ultimate term of a formal dialectics which clothes an unreal fact in the garb first of truth then of a lie denounced as such. This has to be related to a certain mythology of the universal typifying the bourgeois society of which the Novel is a characteristic product; it involves giving to the imaginary the formal guarantee of the real, but while preserving in the sign the ambiguity of a double object, at once believable and false. This operation occurs constantly in the whole of Western art, in which the false is equal to the true, not through any agnosticism or poetic duplicity, but because the true is supposed to contain a germ of the universal, or to put it differently, an essence capable of fecundating by mere reproduction, several orders of things among which some differ by their remoteness and some by their fictitious character.

It is thanks to an expedient of the same kind that the triumphant bourgeoisie of the last century was able to look upon its values as universal and to carry over to sections of society which were absolutely heterogeneous to it all the Names which were parts of its ethos. This is strictly how myths function, and the Novel – and within the Novel, the preterite – are mythological objects in which there is, superimposed upon an immediate intention, a second-order appeal to a corpus of dogmas, or better, to a pedagogy, since what is sought is to impart an essence in the guise of an artefact. In order to grasp the significance of the preterite, we have but to compare the Western art of the novel with a certain Chinese tradition, for instance, in which art lies solely in the perfection with which reality is imitated. But in this tradition no sign, absolutely nothing, must allow any distinction to be drawn between the natural and the artificial objects: this wooden walnut must not impart to me, along with the image of a walnut, the intention of conveying to me the art which gave birth to it. Whereas on the contrary this is what writing does in the novel. Its task is to put the mask in place and at the same time to point it out.

This ambiguous function disclosed in the preterite is found in another fact relating to this type of writing: the third person in the Novel. The reader will perhaps recall a novel by Agatha Christie in which all the invention consisted in concealing the murderer beneath the use of the first person of the narrative. The reader looked for him behind every 'he' in the plot: he was all the time hidden under the 'I'. Agatha Christie knew perfectly well that, in the novel, the 'I' is usually a spectator, and that it is the 'he' who is the actor. Why? The 'he' is a typical novelistic convention; like the narrative tense, it signifies and carries through the action of the novel; if the third person is absent, the novel is powerless to come into being, and even wills its own destruction. The 'he' is a formal manifestation of the myth, and we have just seen that, in the West at least, there is no art which does not point to its own mask. The third person, like the preterite, therefore performs this service for the art of the novel, and supplies its consumers with the security born of a credible fabrication which is yet constantly held up as false.

Less ambiguous, the 'I' is thereby less typical of the novel: it is therefore at the same time the most obvious solution, when the narration remains on this side of convention (Proust's work, for instance, purports to be a mere introduction to Literature), and the most sophisticated, when the 'I' takes its place beyond convention and attempts to destroy it, by conferring on the narrative the spurious naturalness of taking the reader into its confidence (such is the guileful air of some stories by Gide). In the same way the use of the 'he' in a novel involves two opposed systems of ethics: since it represents an unquestioned convention, it attracts the most conformist and the least dissatisfied, as well as those others who have decided that, finally, this convention is necessary to the novelty of their work. In any case, it is the sign of an intelligible pact between society and the author;

but it is also, for the latter, the most important means he has of building the world in the way that he chooses. It is therefore more than a literary experiment: it is a human act which connects creation to History or to existence.

In Balzac for instance, the multiplicity of 'he's', this vast network of characters, slight in terms of solid flesh, but consistent by the duration of their acts, reveals the existence of a world of which History is the first datum. The Balzacian 'he' is not the end-product of a development starting from some transformed and generalized 'I'; it is the original and crude element of the novel, the material, not the outcome, the creative activity: there is no Balzacian history prior to the history of each third person in the novels of Balzac. His 'he' is analogous to Caesar's 'he': the third person here brings about a kind of algebraic state of the action, in which existence plays the smallest possible part, in favour of elements which connect, clarify, or show the tragedy inherent in human relationships. Conversely – or at any rate previously – the function of 'he' in the novel can be that of expressing an existential experience. In many modern novelists the history of the man is identified with the course of the conjugation: starting from an 'I' which is still the form which expresses anonymity most faithfully, man and author little by little win the right to the third person, in proportion as existence becomes fate, and soliloquy becomes a

Novel. Here the appearance of the 'he' is not the starting point of History, it is the end of an effort which has been successful in extracting from a personal world made up of humours and tendencies, a form which is pure, significant, and which therefore vanishes as soon as it is born thanks to the totally conventional and ethereal decor of the third person. This certainly was the course displayed in the first novels of Jean Cayrol whose case can be taken as an exemplar. But whereas in the classics – and we know that where writing is concerned classicism lasts until Flaubert – the withdrawal of the biological person testifies to the establishment of essential man, in novelists such as Cayrol, the invasion of the 'he' is a progressive conquest over the profound darkness of the existential 'I': so true it is that the Novel, identified as it is by its most formal signs, is a gesture of sociability; it establishes Literature as an institution.

Maurice Blanchot has shown, in the case of Kafka, that the elaboration of the impersonal narrative (let us notice, apropos of this term, that the 'third person' is always presented as a negative degree of the person) was an act of fidelity to the essence of language, since the latter naturally tends towards its own destruction. We therefore understand how 'he' is a victory over 'I', inasmuch as it conjures up a state at once more literary and more absent. None the less this victory is ceaselessly threatened: the literary convention of the 'he' is necessary to the belittling of

the person, but runs at every moment the risk of en-
cumbering it with an unexpected density. For Literature is like phosphorus: it shines with its maximum
brilliance at the moment when it attempts to die. But
as, on the other hand, it is an act which necessarily
implies a duration – especially in the Novel – there
can never be any Novel independently of Belles-
Lettres. So that the third person in the Novel is one of
the most obsessive signs of this tragic aspect of writing which was born in the last century, when under
the weight of History, Literature became dissociated
from the society which consumes it. Between the
third person as used by Balzac and that used by
Flaubert, there is a world of difference (that of 1848):
in the former we have a view of History which is
harsh, but coherent and certain of its principles, the
triumph of an order; in the latter, an art which in
order to escape its pangs of conscience either exag-
gerates conventions or frantically attempts to destroy
them. Modernism begins with the search for a Literature which is no longer possible.

Thus we find, in the Novel too, this machinery
directed towards both destruction and resurrection,
and typical of the whole of modern art. What must
be destroyed is duration, that is, the ineffable binding
force running through existence: for order, whether

it be that of poetic flow or of narrative signs, that of
Terror or plausibility, is always a murder in intention. But what reconquers the writer is again duration, for it is impossible to develop a negative within
time, without elaborating a positive art, an order
which must be destroyed anew. So that the greater
modern works linger as long as possible, in a sort of
miraculous stasis, on the threshold of Literature, in
this anticipatory state in which the breadth of life is
given, stretched but not yet destroyed by this crowning phase, an order of signs. For instance, we have the
first person in Proust, whose whole work rests on a
slow and protracted effort towards Literature. We
have Jean Cayrol, whose acquiescence to the Novel
comes only as the very last stage of soliloquy, as if
the literary act, being supremely ambiguous, could be
delivered of a creation consecrated by society, only at
the moment when it has at last succeeded in destroying the existential density of a hitherto meaningless
duration.

The Novel is a Death; it transforms life into
destiny, a memory into a useful act, duration into an
orientated and meaningful time. But this transformation can be accomplished only in full view of society.
It is society which imposes the Novel, that is, a com-
plex of signs, as a transcendence and as the History of
a duration. It is therefore by the obviousness of its
intention, grasped in that of the narrative signs, that
one can recognize the path which, through all the

solemnity of art, binds the writer to society. The preterite and the third person in the Novel are nothing but the fateful gesture with which the writer draws attention to the mask which he is wearing. The whole of Literature can declare *Larvatus prodeo*,* As I walk forward, I point out my mask. Whether we deal with the inhuman experience of the poet, who accepts the most momentous of all breaks, that from the language of society, or with the plausible untruth of the novelist, sincerity here feels a need of the signs of falsehood, and of conspicuous falsehood in order to last and to be consumed. Writing is the product, and ultimately the source, of this ambiguity. This specialized language, the use of which gives the writer a glorious but none the less superintended function, evinces a kind of servitude, invisible at first, which characterizes any responsibility. Writing, free in its beginnings, is finally the bond which links the writer to a History which is itself in chains: society stamps upon him the unmistakable signs of art so as to draw him along the more inescapably in its own process of alienation.

* *Larvatus prodeo* was the motto of Descartes.

IS THERE ANY POETIC
WRITING?

In the classical period, prose and poetry are quantities, their difference can be measured; they are neither more nor less separated than two different numbers, contiguous like them, but dissimilar because of the very difference in their magnitudes. If I use the word prose for a minimal form of speech, the most economical vehicle for thought, and if I use the letters a, b, c for certain attributes of language, which are useless but decorative, such as metre, rhyme or the ritual of images, all the linguistic surface will be accounted for in M. Jourdain's* double equation:

$$Poetry = Prose + a + b + c$$
$$Prose = Poetry - a - b - c$$

whence it clearly follows that Poetry is always different from Prose. But this difference is not one of essence, it is one of quantity. It does not, therefore, jeopardize the unity of language, which is an article of classical dogma. One may effect a different dosage in manner of speech, according to the social occasion: here, prose or rhetoric, there, poetry or precosity, in

* Molière's *Bourgeois Gentilhomme.*

accordance with a whole ritual of expression laid down by good society, but there remains everywhere a single language, which reflects the eternal categories of the mind. Classical poetry is felt to be merely an ornamental variation of prose, the fruit of an *art* (that is, a technique), never a different language, or the product of a particular sensibility. Any poetry is then only the decorative equation, whether allusive or forced, of a possible prose which is latent, virtually and potentially, in any conceivable manner of expression. 'Poetic', in the days of classicism, never evokes any particular domain, any particular depth of feeling, any special coherence, or separate universe, but only an individual handling of a verbal technique, that of 'expressing oneself' according to rules more artistic, therefore more sociable, than those of conversation, in other terms, the technique of projecting out an inner thought, springing fully armed from the Mind, a speech which is made more socially acceptable by virtue of the very conspicuousness of its conventions.

We know that nothing of this structure remains in modern poetry, which springs not from Baudelaire but from Rimbaud, unless it is in cases where one takes up again, in a revised traditional mode, the formal imperatives of classical poetry: henceforth, poets give to their speech the status of a closed Nature, which covers both the function and the structure of language. Poetry is then no longer a Prose either ornamental or shorn of liberties. It is a quality *sui generis* and without antecedents. It is no longer an attribute but a substance, and therefore it can very well renounce signs, since it carries its own nature within itself, and does not need to signal its identity outwardly: poetic language and prosaic language are sufficiently separate to be able to dispense with the very signs of their difference.

Furthermore, the alleged relations between thought and language are reversed; in classical art, a ready-made thought generates an utterance which 'expresses' or 'translates' it. Classical thought is devoid of duration, classical poetry has it only in such degree as is necessary to its technical arrangement. In modern poetics, on the contrary, words produce a kind of formal continuum from which there gradually emanates an intellectual or emotional density which would have been impossible without them; speech is then the solidified time of a more spiritual gestation, during which the 'thought' is prepared, installed little by little by the contingency of words. This verbal luck, which will bring down the ripe fruit of a meaning, presupposes therefore a poetic time which is no longer that of a 'fabrication', but that of a possible adventure, the meeting-point of a sign and an intention. Modern poetry is opposed to classical art by a difference which involves the whole structure of language, without leaving between those two types of poetry anything in common except the same sociological intention.

The economy of classical language (Prose and Poetry) is relational, which means that in it words are abstracted as much as possible in the interest of relationships. In it, no word has a density by itself, it is hardly the sign of a thing, but rather the means of conveying a connection. Far from plunging into an inner reality consubstantial to its outer configuration, it extends, as soon as it is uttered, towards other words, so as to form a superficial chain of intentions. A glance at the language of mathematics will perhaps enable us to grasp the relational nature of classical prose and poetry: we know that in mathematical language, not only is each quantity provided with a sign, but also that the relations between these quantities are themselves transcribed, by means of a sign expressing operative equality or difference. It may be said that the whole movement of mathematical flow derives from an explicit reading of its relations. The language of classicism is animated by an analogous, although of course less rigid, movement: its 'words', neutralized, made absent by rigorous recourse to a tradition which dessicates their freshness, avoid the phonetic or semantic accident which would concentrate the flavour of language at one point and halt its

intellectual momentum in the interest of an un-
equally distributed enjoyment. The classical flow is a
succession of elements whose density is even; it is exposed to the same emotional pressure, and relieves
those elements of any tendency towards an individual
meaning appearing at all invented. The poetic vocabulary itself is one of usage, not of invention: images in
it are recognizable in a body; they do not exist in
isolation; they are due to long custom, not to individual creation. The function of the classical poet
is not therefore to find new words, with more body
or more brilliance, but to follow the order of an
ancient ritual, to perfect the symmetry or the conciseness of a relation, to bring a thought exactly
within the compass of a metre. Classical conceits involve relations, not words: they belong to an art of
expression, not of invention. The words, here, do not,
as they later do, thanks to a kind of violent and unexpected abruptness, reproduce the depth and singularity of an individual experience; they are spread out
to form a surface, according to the exigencies of an
elegant or decorative purpose. They delight us because of the formulation which brings them together,
not because of their own power or beauty.

True, classical language does not reach the functional perfection of the relational network of mathematics: relations are not signified, in it, by any
special signs, but only by accidents of form and dis-
position. It is the restraint of the words in itself, their

alignment, which achieves the relational nature of classical discourse. Overworked in a restricted number of ever-similar relations, classical words are on the way to becoming an algebra where rhetorical figures of speech, clichés, function as virtual linking devices; they have lost their density and gained a more interrelated state of speech; they operate in the manner of chemical valences, outlining a verbal area full of symmetrical connections, junctions and networks from which arise, without the respite afforded by wonder, fresh intentions towards signification. Hardly have the fragments of classical discourse yielded their meaning than they become messengers or harbingers, carrying ever further a meaning which refuses to settle within the depths of a word, but tries instead to spread widely enough to become a total gesture of intellection, that is, of communication.

Now the distortion to which Hugo tried to subject the alexandrine, which is of all meters the most interrelational, already contains the whole future of modern poetry, since what is attempted is to eliminate the intention to establish relationships and to produce instead an explosion of words. For modern poetry, since it must be distinguished from classical poetry and from any type of prose, destroys the spontaneously functional nature of language, and leaves standing only its lexical basis. It retains only the outward shape of relationships, their music, but not their reality. The Word shines forth above a line of relationships emptied of their content, grammar is bereft of its purpose, it becomes prosody and is no longer anything but an inflexion which lasts only to present the Word. Connections are not properly speaking abolished, they are merely reserved areas, a parody of themselves, and this void is necessary for the density of the Word to rise out of a magic vacuum, like a sound and a sign devoid of background, like 'fury and mystery'.

In classical speech, connections lead the word on, and at once carry it towards a meaning which is an ever-deferred project; in modern poetry, connections are only an extension of the word, it is the Word which is 'the dwelling place', it is rooted like a *fons et origo* in the prosody of functions, which are perceived but unreal. Here, connections only fascinate, and it is the Word which gratifies and fulfills like the sudden revelation of a truth. To say that this truth is of a poetic order is merely to say that the Word in poetry can never be untrue, because it is a whole; it shines with an infinite freedom and prepares to radiate towards innumerable uncertain and possible connections. Fixed connections being abolished, the word is left only with a vertical project, it is like a monolith, or a pillar which plunges into a totality of meanings, reflexes and recollections: it is a sign which stands. The poetic word is here an act without immediate past, without environment, and which holds forth only the dense shadow of reflexes from all sources which are associated with it. Thus under each Word in modern poetry there lies a sort of existential geology, in which is gathered the total content of the Name, instead of a chosen content as in classical prose and poetry. The Word is no longer guided *in advance* by the general intention of a socialized discourse; the consumer of poetry, deprived of the guide of selective connections, encounters the Word frontally, and receives it as an absolute quantity, accompanied by all its possible associations. The Word, here, is encyclopaedic, it contains simultaneously all the acceptations from which a relational discourse might have required it to choose. It therefore achieves a state which is possible only in the dictionary or in poetry – places where the noun can live without its article – and is reduced to a sort of zero degree, pregnant with all past and future specifications. The word here has a generic form; it is a category. Each poetic word is thus an unexpected object, a Pandora's box from which fly out all the potentialities of language; it is therefore produced and consumed with a peculiar curiosity, a kind of sacred relish. This Hunger of the Word, common to the whole of modern poetry, makes poetic speech terrible and inhuman. It initiates a discourse full of gaps and full of lights, filled with absences and over-nourishing signs, without foresight or stability of intention, and thereby so opposed to the social function of language that merely to have recourse to a discontinuous speech is to open the door to all that stands above Nature.

For what does the rational economy of classical language mean, if not that Nature is a plenum, that it can be possessed, that it does not shy away or cover itself in shadows, but is in its entirety subjected to the toils of language? Classical language is always reducible to a persuasive continuum, it postulates the possibility of dialogue, it establishes a universe in which men are not alone, where words never have the terrible weight of things, where speech is always a meeting with the others. Classical language is a bringer of euphoria because it is immediately social. There is no genre, no written work of classicism which does not suppose a collective consumption, akin to speech; classical literary art is an object which circulates among several persons brought together on a class basis; it is a product conceived for oral transmission, for a consumption regulated by the contingencies of society: it is essentially a spoken language, in spite of its strict codification.

We have seen that on the contrary modern poetry destroyed relationships in language and reduced discourse to words as static things. This implies a reversal in our knowledge of Nature. The interrupted flow of the new poetic language initiates a discon-

tinuous Nature, which is revealed only piecemeal. At
the very moment when the withdrawal of functions
obscures the relations existing in the world, the
object in discourse assumes an exalted place : modern
poetry is a poetry of the object. In it, Nature becomes
a fragmented space, made of objects solitary and terrible, because the links between them are only
potential. Nobody chooses for them a privileged
meaning, or a particular use, or some service; nobody
imposes a hierarchy on them, nobody reduces them
to the manifestation of a mental behaviour, or of an
intention, of some evidence of tenderness, in short.
The bursting upon us of the poetic word then insti-
tutes an absolute object; Nature becomes a succession
of verticalities, of objects, suddenly standing erect,
and filled with all their possibilities : one of these can
be only a landmark in an unfulfilled, and thereby
terrible, world. These unrelated objects – words
adorned with all the violence of their irruption, the
vibration of which, though wholly mechanical,
strangely affects the next word, only to die out immediately – these poetic words exclude men : there is
no humanism of modern poetry. This erect discourse
is full of terror, that is to say, it relates man not to
other men, but to the most inhuman images in
Nature : heaven, hell, holiness, childhood, madness,
pure matter, etc.

At such a point, it is hardly possible to speak of a
poetic mode of writing, for this is a language in

which a violent drive towards autonomy destroys any ethical scope. The verbal gesture here aims at modifying Nature, it is the approach of a demiurge; it is not an attitude of the conscience but an act of coercion. Such, at least, is the language of those modern poets who carry their intention to the limit, and assume Poetry not as a spiritual exercise, a state of the soul or a placing of oneself in a situation, but as the splendour and freshness of a dream language. For such poets, it is as vain to speak about a mode of writing as of poetic feeling. Modern Poetry, in Char, for instance, is beyond this diffuse tone, this precious *aura*, which *are*, indeed, a mode of writing, usually termed poetic feeling. There is no objection to speaking of a poetic mode of writing concerning the classical writers and their epigones, or even concerning poetic prose in the manner of Gide's *Fruits of the Earth*, in which Poetry is in fact a certain linguistic ethos. In both cases, the mode of writing soaks up the style, and we can imagine that for people living in the seventeenth century, it was not easy to perceive an *immediate* difference between Racine and Pradon (and even less a difference of a poetic kind), just as it is not easy for a modern reader to pass judgment on those contemporary poets who use the same uniform and indecisive poetic mode of writing, because for them Poetry is a *climate* which means, essentially, a linguistic convention. But when the poetic language radically questions Nature by virtue of its very structure, without any resort to the content of the discourse and without falling back on some ideology, there is no mode of writing left, there are only styles, thanks to which man turns his back on society and confronts the world of objects without going through any of the forms of History or of social life.

Part Two

THE TRIUMPH AND BREAK-UP
OF BOURGEOIS WRITING

There is, in pre-classical Literature, the appearance
of a variety of modes of writing; but this variety
seems far less wide if one puts these linguistic problems in terms of structure and not in terms of art.
Aesthetically, the sixteenth and the beginning of the
seventeenth centuries show a fairly lavish profusion
of literary languages because men are still engaged in
the task of getting to know Nature, and not yet in
that of giving expression to man's essence. On these
grounds, the encyclopaedic writing of Rabelais, or the
precious writing of Corneille – to take only such
typical moments – have as a common form a language in which ornaments are not yet ritualistic but
are in themselves a method of investigation applied
to the whole surface of the world. This is what gives
to this pre-classical writing the genuine appearance of
many-sidedness, and the euphoria which comes from
freedom. For a modern reader, the impression of
variety is all the stronger since the French tongue
seems to be still experimenting with unstable structures, and since it has not yet fully settled on the

character of its syntax or the laws governing the increase of its vocabulary. To take up again the distinction between a language and a mode of writing, we can say that until around 1650, French literature had not yet gone further than the problematics of the language, and that by this very fact, it was as yet unaware of modes of writing. For as long as a tongue is still uncertain about its very structure, an ethics of language is impossible; modes of writing appear only when the language, being established on a national scale, becomes a kind of negativity, a line which separates what is forbidden from what is allowed, without asking itself any more questions about its origins or the justifications for such a taboo. By creating an intemporal reason working through the language, the classical grammarians have relieved the French from any linguistic problem, and this purified language has become a mode of writing, that is, a language to which is attached a value, and which is given immediately as universal by very virtue of the historical situation.

The diversity of the 'genres' and the varying rhythms of styles within the framework of classical dogma are aesthetic, not structural, data; neither must deceive us: there was indeed one and only one mode of writing, both instrumental and ornamental, at the disposal of French society during the whole period when bourgeois ideology conquered and triumphed. Instrumental, since form was supposed to be at the service of content, just as an algebraic equation is at the service of an operational process; ornamental, since the instrument in question was embellished with accidental features external to its function, and unselfconsciously borrowed from Tradition, so that this bourgeois mode of writing, taken in turn by different writers, was never shunned for its pedigree, since it was only a felicitous backcloth against which the act of thought was thrown into relief. Classical writers have indeed themselves faced problems of form, but the point at issue was in no way the plurality and meaning of modes of writing, still less the structure of the language. The only thing in question was rhetoric, namely the ordering of discourse in such a way as to persuade. To a single bourgeois writing there corresponded, therefore, several rhetorics; conversely, it was at the very moment when treatises on rhetoric aroused no more interest, towards the middle of the nineteenth century, that classical writing ceased to be universal and that modern modes of writing came into being.

This classical writing is, needless to say, a class writing. Born in the seventeenth century in the group which was closest to the people in power, shaped by force of dogmatic decisions, promptly ridding itself of all grammatical turns of speech forged by the spontaneous subjectivity of ordinary people, and drilled, on the contrary, for a task of definition, bourgeois writing was first presented, with the cynicism

customary in the first flush of political victory, as
the language of a privileged minority. In 1647,
Vaugelas recommends classical writing as a *de facto*,
not a *de jure*, state of affairs; clear expression is still
only court usage. In 1660, on the contrary, in the
Grammaire of Port-Royal for instance, classical language wears a universal look, and clarity has become
a value. In actual fact, clarity is a purely rhetorical
attribute, not a quality of language in general, which
is possible at all times and in all places, but only the
ideal appendage to a certain type of discourse, that
which is given over to a permanent intention to persuade. It is because the pre-bourgeoisie of the *Ancien
Régime* and the post-revolutionary bourgeoisie, using
the same mode of writing, have developed an essen-
tialist mythology of man, that classical writing, unified and universal, renounced all hesitancy in favour
of a continuum in which every fragment was a
choice, that is, the radical elimination of all virtuali-
ties in language. Political authority, spiritualistic
dogmatism, and unity in the language of classicism
are therefore various aspects of the same historical
movement.

So it is no wonder that the Revolution changed
nothing in bourgeois writing, and that there is only a
slight difference between the writing of, say, Fénelon
and Mérimée. This is because bourgeois ideology remained intact until 1848 without being in the least
shaken by a Revolution which gave the bourgeoisie

political and social power, although not the intellectual power, which it had long held. From Laclos to Stendhal, bourgeois writing needed only to resume its continuity after the short interruption of troubled times. And the romantic revolution, so theoretically committed to the overthrow of traditional forms, in the event, stuck prudently to the writing of its ideology. A few concessions such as the mixing of genres and words enabled it to preserve the main feature of classical language, namely, instrumentality. True, this instrument comes more and more to the fore (notably in Chateaubriand), but all in all it is still an instrument, used without aloofness, and not yet, as a language, conscious of solitude. Hugo alone, by evolving, out of the concrete dimensions of his own personal time and space, a particular and thematic use of language, which could no longer be understood with reference to a tradition, but only in the light of the formidable reality lying behind his own existence, Hugo alone, then, through the weight of his style, was able to exert some pressure on classical writing and bring it to the verge of disintegration. This is why contempt for Hugo still serves to bolster up the self-same writing in eighteenth century taste, which witnessed the heyday of the bourgeoisie, and remains the norm of 'accepted' French, a carefully closed language, separated from society by the whole body of the literary myth, a consecrated mode of writing used indiscriminately by the most heterogeneous writers as an austere duty or a connoisseur's relish, a tabernacle of this awe-inspiring mystery: French Literature.

Now the 1850s bring the concurrence of three new and important facts in History: the demographic expansion in Europe, the replacement of textile by heavy industry, that is, the birth of modern capitalism, the scission (completed by the revolution of June 1848) of French society into three mutually hostile classes, bringing the definitive ruin of liberal illusions. These circumstances put the bourgeoisie into a new historical situation. Until then, it was bourgeois ideology itself which gave the measure of the universal by fulfilling it unchallenged. The bourgeois writer, sole judge of other people's woes and without anyone else to gaze on him, was not torn between his social condition and his intellectual vocation. Henceforth, this very ideology appears merely as one among many possible others; the universal escapes it, since transcending itself would mean condemning itself; the writer falls a prey to ambiguity, since his consciousness no longer accounts for the whole of his condition. Thus is born a tragic predicament peculiar to Literature.

It is at this moment that modes of writing begin to multiply. Each one, henceforth, be it the highly wrought, populist, neutral or colloquial, sets itself up as the initial act whereby the writer acknowledges or repudiates his bourgeois condition. Each one is an attempt to find a solution to this Orphean problematics of modern Form : writers without Literature. For the last hundred years, Flaubert, Mallarmé, Rimbaud, the Goncourt brothers, the Surrealists, Queneau, Sartre, Blanchot or Camus, have outlined – indeed are still outlining – certain ways of integrating, disrupting or naturalizing literary language; but what is at stake is not some adventure of literary form, some success in rhetorical achievement or some bold use of vocabulary. Whenever the writer assembles a network of words it is the existence of Literature itself which is called into question; what modernity allows us to read in the plurality of modes of writing, is the blind alley which is its own History.

STYLE AS CRAFTSMANSHIP

'Form is costly,' Valéry would answer when asked why he did not publish his lectures at the Collège de France. Yet there has been a whole period, that of triumphant bourgeois writing, when form cost about the same price as thought. It is true that attention was paid to its conciseness and order, and to its euphemistic grace, but form was all the cheaper since the writer was using a ready-made instrument, the working of which was handed down unchanged without anyone being obsessed with novelty. Form was not seen as a possession; the universality of classical language derived from the fact that language was common property, and that thought alone bore the weight of being different. We might say that throughout this period, form had a usage value.

Now we have seen that around 1850, Literature begins to face a problem of self-justification; it is now on the point of seeking alibis for itself; and precisely because the shadow of a doubt begins to be cast on its usage, a whole class of writers anxious to assume to the full the responsibility of their tradition is about to put the work-value of writing in place of its usage-value. Writing is now to be saved not by virtue of what it exists for, but thanks to the work it has cost. There begins now to grow up an image of the writer as a craftsman who shuts himself away in some legendary place, like a workman operating at home, and who roughs out, cuts, polishes and sets his form exactly as a jeweller extracts art from his material, devoting to his work regular hours of solitary effort. Writers like Gautier (past master in Belles-Lettres), Flaubert (grinding away at his sentences at Croisset), Valéry (in his room at the crack of dawn) or Gide (standing at his desk like a carpenter at his bench) form a kind of guild of French Literature, in which work expended on form is the sign and the property of a corporation. Labour replaces genius as a value, so to speak; there is a kind of ostentation in claiming to labour long and lovingly over the form of one's work. There even arises, sometimes, a preciosity of conciseness (for labouring at one's material usually means reducing it), in contrast to the great preciosity of the baroque era (that of Corneille, for instance). For the latter expresses a knowledge of Nature which necessitates a broadening of the language; but the former, trying to evolve an aristocratic literary style, lays down the conditions for a historical crisis, destined to begin on the day when an aesthetic aim no longer suffices to justify the convention which this anachronistic language represents, that is, on the day when History has brought about an obvious disjunction between the social vocation of the writer and the instrument which he has inherited from Tradition.

Flaubert it was who most methodically laid the foundations for this conception of writing as craft. Before him, the existence of the bourgeois was a picturesque or exotic phenomenon; bourgeois ideology supplied the norm of the universal and, postulating that pure man existed as such, could experience a sense of well-being as it contemplated the bourgeois as a spectacle in no way commensurate with itself. Whereas for Flaubert the bourgeois state is an incurable ill which sticks to the writer, and which he can cure only by assuming it clear-sightedly – which is of the essence of tragic feeling. This bourgeois Necessity which characterizes Frédéric Moreau, Emma Bovary, Bouvard and Pécuchet, requires, as soon as it is squarely faced and accepted, an art which is equally the bearer of a necessity, and armed with a Law. Flaubert founded a normative writing which – and this is a paradox – includes technical rules which can reveal pathos. On the one hand, he builds his narrative by a succession of essences, and not at all by following a phenomenological order (as Proust later does); he finalizes the uses of verbal tenses according to a convention, so as to make them perform the function of *signs* of Literature, in the manner of an art drawing attention to its very artificiality; he elaborates a rhythm of the written word which creates a sort of incantation and which, quite unlike the rules of spoken eloquence, appeals to a sixth, purely literary, sense, the private property of producers and consumers of Literature. And on the other hand this code of literary labour, this sum of exercises related to the writer's work, keep up a wisdom, so to speak, which is also touched with sadness, and openness too, since the art of Flaubert points to its mask as it moves forward. What this Gregorian codification of literary language aimed at was, if not the reconciliation of the writer to a universal condition, at least the conferment upon him of the responsibility for his form, the transmutation of the writing handed down to him by History into an *art;* in other words, into an obvious convention, a sincere pact which would enable man to adopt a position he was familiar with in a nature still made of ill-matched realities. The writer then gives to society a self-confessed art, whose rules are visible to all, and in exchange society is able to accept the writer. Baudelaire, for instance, insisted on tracing the admirable prosaicness of his poetry back to Gautier, to a kind of fetish of *highly wrought* form, situated no doubt outside pragmatic bourgeois activity, but inserted into an order of familiar tasks, under the eye of a society which recognized in it not its dreams but its methods. Since Literature could not be vanquished by its own weapons, was it not better to accept it openly, and, being condemned to this literary hard labour, to 'do good work' in it? So the 'Flaubertization' of writing redeems all writers at a stroke, partly because the least exacting abandon themselves to it without qualms, and partly because the purest return to it as to an acknowledgment of their fate.

WRITING AND REVOLUTION

The conception of style as craftsmanship has produced a mode of sub-writing, derived from Flaubert, but adapted to the aims of the Naturalist school. This writing, which is that of Maupassant, Zola and Daudet and which could be called the realist mode of writing, is a combination of the formal signs of Literature (preterite, indirect speech, the rhythm of written language) and of the no less formal signs of realism (incongruous snippets of popular speech, strong language or dialect words, etc.), so that no mode of writing was more artificial than that which set out to give the most accurate description of Nature. This is no mere stylistic failure but one of theory as well: there is, in the Naturalist aesthetic, a convention of the real, just as there is a fabrication in its writing. The paradox is that the abasement of subjects has not in the least entailed the unobtrusiveness of form. Neutral writing is a late phenomenon to be invented only much later than Realism by authors like Camus, less under the impulse of an aesthetics of escape than in search of a mode of writing which might at last achieve innocence. The writing of Real-

ism is far from being neutral, it is on the contrary
loaded with the most spectacular signs of fabrication.

Thus, when it became degraded by abandoning the
insistence on a verbal Nature openly foreign to reality, while still not pretending to revert to the language of social Nature – as did Queneau later – the
Naturalist school paradoxically evolved a mechanical
art which flaunted the signs of literary convention
with an ostentation hitherto unknown. In Flaubertian
writing a spell was gradually woven, and it is still
possible to lose oneself reading Flaubert as if one
were in a nature full of echoing voices in which signs
are rather persuasive than expressive. Whereas the
writing of Realism can never be convincing; it is condemned to mere description by virtue of this dualistic
dogma which ordains that there shall only ever be
one optimum form to 'express' a reality as inert as an
object, on which the writer can have no power except through his art of arranging the signs.

These authors without a style – Maupassant, Zola,
Daudet and their epigones – have used a mode of
writing which represented for them a means both of
rescuing and displaying the craftsmanship which they
fancied they had expelled from a purely passive
aesthetic. Maupassant's declarations on the labour
associated with form are well known, as are all the

naive devices of his school, whereby the natural sentence is transformed into an artificial one meant to bear witness to its purely literary purpose, which means, in this instance, to what it cost in labour. We know that according to Maupassant's stylistics, the artistic intention is the preserve of syntax, the vocabulary being meant to stay on this side of Literature. To write well – now the sole sign of literary reality – means naively to shift the place of a predicate, to 'set off' a word while being hopeful of obtaining by this means an 'expressive' rhythm. But expressiveness is a myth : it is only the convention of expressiveness.

This conventional mode of writing has always been a happy hunting ground for study in schools, where the value of a text is assessed by the obvious signs of the labour it has cost. Now nothing is more spectacular than attempting to combine predicates, as a workman adjusts some delicate mechanism. What pedants admire in the writing of a Maupassant or a Daudet is a literary sign at last detached from its content, which posits Literature unambiguously as a category without any relation to other languages, and in so doing establishes an ideal intelligibility of things. Between a proletariat excluded from all culture, and an intelligentsia which has already begun to question Literature itself, the verage public produced by primary and secondary schools, namely lower-middle class, roughly speaking, will therefore find in the artistic-realistic mode of writing – which is that of a good proportion of commercial novels – the image *par excellence* of a Literature which has all the striking and intelligible signs of its identity. In this case the function of the writer is not so much to create a work as to supply a Literature which can be seen from afar.

This lower-middle-class mode of writing has been taken up by communist writers because, for the time being, the artistic norms of the proletariat cannot be different from those of the *petite bourgeoisie* (a fact which indeed agrees with their doctrine), and because the very dogma of socialist realism necessarily entails the adoption of a conventional mode of writing, to which is assigned the task of signifying in a conspicuous way a content which is powerless to impose itself without a form to identify it. Thus is understood the paradox whereby the communist mode of writing makes multiple use of the grossest signs of Literature, and far from breaking with a form which is after all typically bourgeois – or which was such in the past, at least – goes on assuming without reservation the formal preoccupations of the *petit-bourgeois* art of writing (which is moreover accredited with the communist public, thanks to the essays done in the primary school).

French socialist realism has therefore taken up the mode of writing of bourgeois realism, mechanizing without restraint all the intentional signs of art. Here are for instance a few lines of a novel by Garaudy: ' ... with torso bent, he launched himself at full speed on the keyboard of the linotype ... joy sang in his muscles, his fingers danced, light and powerful ... the poisoned vapour of antimony ... made his temples pulsate and his arteries hammer, fanning his strength, his anger and his mental exaltation.' We see that nothing here is given without metaphor, for it must be laboriously borne home to the reader that 'it is well written' (that is, that what he is consuming is Literature). These metaphors, which seize the very slightest verb, in no way indicate the intention of an individual Humour trying to convey the singularity of a sensation, but only a literary stamp which 'places' a language, just as a label tells us the price of an article.

'To type', 'to throb' or 'to be happy for the first time', is real, not Realist language; for Literature to come into existence one must write: 'to strum on the linotype', 'his arteries hammered ... ' or 'he was clutching the first happy moment of his life.' Realist writing can therefore lead only to a species of preciosity. Garaudy writes: 'At the end of each line, the thin arm of the linotype plucked away a handful of dancing matrices,' or 'Each caress of his fingers awakes and sends a shiver through the joyous chime of copper matrices which fall into the grooves in a tinkling shower of notes.' This jargon is really no different from that of Cathos and Magdelon.*

Of course, we must allow for mediocrity; in the case of Garaudy, it is impressive. In André Stil, we shall find devices which are much more discreet but which do not escape the rules of artistic-realist writing. Here metaphors do not pretend to be more than a cliché, almost fully integrated to real language, and signifying Literature at no great cost: 'crystal clear', 'hands white as parchment with the cold', etc. The preciosity is driven from the vocabulary into the syntax, and it is the artificial arrangement of the predicates, as in Maupassant, which establishes the text as Literature ('with one hand, she lifts up the knees, her body bent'). This language, steeped in conventionality, presents reality only in inverted commas: would-be working-class words, slipshod turns of speech are used together with a purely literary syntax: 'That's true, it's kicking up a shindy all right, that wind!', or even better: 'Their bérets and caps buffeted in the wind above their eyes, they look at each other pretty quizzically' (in which the colloquial 'pretty' follows an absolute participle, a form of speech totally unknown in spoken language). Needless to say, one must set Aragon in a class apart, since his literary antecedents are of a quite different kind, and since he has preferred to mix in with realist writing a slight

* Cathos and Magdelon are Molière's *Précieuses Ridicules*.

eighteenth century colour, adding a little Laclos to
Zola.

Perhaps there is, in this well-behaved writing of
revolutionaries, a feeling of powerlessness to create
forthwith a free writing. Perhaps also the fact that
only bourgeois writers can feel that bourgeois writing
is compromised: the disintegration of literary language was a phenomenon which owed its existence
to consciousness, not to revolution. And certainly the
fact that Stalinist ideology imposes a terror before all
problematics, even and above all revolutionary:
bourgeois writing is thought to be all in all less
dangerous than its being put on trial. This is why
communist writers are the only ones who go on im-
perturbably keeping alive a bourgeois writing which
bourgeois writers have themselves condemned long
ago, since the day when they felt it was endangered
by the impostures of their own ideology, namely, the
day when Marxism was thereby justified.

WRITING AND SILENCE

Craftsmanlike writing, since it lies within the bourgeois heritage, does not disturb any order; although deprived of other battles, the writer retains a passion which provides him with sufficient justification : the bringing forth of form. If he renounces the task of setting free a new literary language, he can at least enhance the existing one with new intentions, conceits, purple patches or archaisms, and create another, which is rich and mortal. This great traditional writing, that of Gide, Valéry, Montherlant, even Breton, means that form, through the weight of its unusual posturing, is a value which transcends History, in the same way as a ritual language of priests.

Other writers have thought that they could exorcize this sacred writing only by dislocating it. They have therefore undermined literary language, they have ceaselessly exploded the ever-renewed husk of clichés, of habits, of the formal past of the writer; in a chaos of forms and a wilderness of words they hoped they would achieve an object wholly delivered of History, and find again the freshness of a pristine state of language. But such upheavals end up by leaving their own tracks and creating their own laws. The threat of becoming a Fine Art is a fate which hangs over any language not based exclusively on the speech of society. In a perpetual flight forward from a disorderly syntax, the disintegration of language can only lead to the silence of writing. The final agraphia of Rimbaud or of some Surrealists (who *ipso facto* fell into oblivion), this poignant self-destruction of Literature, teaches us that for some writers, language, the first and last way out of the literary myth, finally restores what it had hoped to avoid, that there is no writing which can be lastingly revolutionary, and that any silence of form can escape imposture only by complete abandonment of communication. Mallarmé, the Hamlet of writing, as it were, well represents this precarious moment of History in which literary language persists only the better to sing the necessity of its death. Mallarmé's typographical agraphia seeks to create around rarefied words an empty zone in which speech, liberated from its guilty social overtones, may, by some happy contrivance, no longer reverberate. The word, dissociated from the husk of habitual clichés, and from the technical reflexes of the writer, is then freed from responsibility in relation to all possible context; it appears in one brief act, which, being devoid of reflections, declares its solitude, and therefore its innocence. This art has the very structure of suicide: in it, silence is a homogeneous poetic time which traps the

word between two layers and sets it off less as a fragment of a cryptogram than as a light, a void, a
murder, a freedom. (We know all that this hypothesis
of Mallarmé as a murderer of language owes to
Maurice Blanchot.) This language of Mallarmé's is
like Orpheus who can save what he loves only by
renouncing it, and who, just the same, cannot resist
glancing round a little; it is Literature brought to the
gates of the Promised Land: a world without Literature, but one to which writers would nevertheless
have to bear witness.

In this same attempt towards disengaging literary
language, here is another solution: to create a colourless writing, freed from all bondage to a pre-ordained
state of language. A simile borrowed from linguistics
will perhaps give a fairly accurate idea of this new
phenomenon; we know that some linguists establish
between the two terms of a polar opposition (such as
singular-plural, preterite-present) the existence of a
third term, called a neutral term or zero element:
thus between the subjunctive and the imperative
moods, the indicative is according to them an amodal
form. Proportionately speaking, writing at the zero
degree is basically in the indicative mood, or if you
like, amodal; it would be accurate to say that it is a
journalist's writing, if it were not precisely the case

that journalism develops, in general, optative or imperative (that is, emotive) forms. The new neutral writing takes its place in the midst of all those ejaculations and judgments, without becoming involved in any of them; it consists precisely in their absence. But this absence is complete, it implies no refuge, no secret; one cannot therefore say that it is an impassive mode of writing; rather, that it is innocent. The aim here is to go beyond Literature by entrusting one's fate to a sort of basic speech, equally far from living languages and from literary language proper. This transparent form of speech, initiated by Camus's *Outsider*, achieves a style of absence which is almost an ideal absence of style; writing is then reduced to a sort of negative mood in which the social or mythical characters of a language are abolished in favour of a neutral and inert state of form; thus thought remains wholly responsible, without being overlaid by a secondary commitment of form to a History not its own. If Flaubert's writing enshrines a Law, if that of Mallarmé postulates a silence, and if others, those of Proust, Céline, Queneau, Prévert, each in its own way, is founded on the existence of a social nature, if all these modes of writing imply an opacity of form and presuppose a problematic of language and society, thus establishing speech as an object which must receive treatment at the hands of a craftsman, a magician or a scriptor, but not by an intellectual, then neutral writing in fact rediscovers the primary

77

condition of classical art: instrumentality. But this time, form as an instrument is no longer at the service of a triumphant ideology; it is the mode of a new situation of the writer, the way a certain silence has of existing; it deliberately forgoes any elegance or ornament, for these two dimensions would reintroduce Time into writing, and this is a derivative power which sustains History. If the writing is really neutral, and if language, instead of being a cumbersome and recalcitrant act, reaches the state of a pure equation, which is no more tangible than an algebra when it confronts the innermost part of man, then Literature is vanquished, the problematics of mankind is uncovered and presented without elaboration, the writer becomes irretrievably honest. Unfortunately, nothing is more fickle than a colourless writing; mechanical habits are developed in the very place where freedom existed, a network of set forms hem in more and more the pristine freshness of discourse, a mode of writing appears afresh in lieu of an indefinite language. The writer, taking his place as a 'classic', becomes the slavish imitator of his original creation, society demotes his writing to a mere manner, and returns him a prisoner to his own formal myths.

WRITING AND SPEECH

A little more than a hundred years ago, writers were for the most part unaware that there were several ways – and very different ones – of speaking French. Around 1830, at the time when the bourgeoisie found good-humoured entertainment in everything situated on the fringe of its own preserve, namely in that inconsiderable portion of society which it was willing to share with bohemians, concierges and pickpockets, there began to find their way into literary language proper a few extraneous scraps lifted from inferior forms of language, provided they were suitably eccentric (otherwise they would have been a source of danger). These picturesque jargons embellished Literature without threatening its structure. Balzac, Süe, Monnier, Hugo found enjoyment in reinstating a few really aberrant forms of pronunciation and vocabulary : thieves' argot, country dialects, German jargon, or the lingo of the concierges. But this social speech, which was a kind of theatrical costume hung on to an essence, never involved the speaker as a total person; the mechanism of the passions went on functioning over and above the speech.

It was perhaps necessary to wait for Proust to see the writer fuse certain men totally with their language, and present his creatures only through that solid and colourful guise, their way of speaking. While Balzac's creatures, for instance, are easily reducible to the power relations of the society of which they are, so to speak, the algebraic expressions, a character of Proust materializes into the opacity of a particular language, and it is really at this level that his whole historical situation – his profession, his class, his wealth, his heredity, his bodily frame – is integrated and ordered. In this way, Literature begins to know society as a Nature, the phenomena of which it might perhaps be able to reproduce. During such moments when the writer follows languages which are really spoken, no longer for the sake of picturesqueness, but as essential objects which fully account for the whole content of society, writing takes as the locus of its reflexes the real speech of men. Literature no longer implies pride or escape, it begins to become a lucid act of giving information; as if it had first to learn the particulars of social differences by reproducing them. It takes it upon itself to give an immediate account, as a preliminary to any other message, of the situation of men immured by the language of their class, their region, their profession, their heredity or their history.

Understood in this way, literary language founded on social speech never gets rid of a descriptive virtue

which limits it, since the universality of a language –
in the present state of society – is a fact concerning
hearing, and not speaking. Within a national norm
such as French, forms of expression differ in different
groups, and every man is a prisoner of his language:
outside his class, the first word he speaks is a sign
which places him as a whole and proclaims his whole
personal history. The man is put on show and delivered up by his language, betrayed by a formal
reality which is beyond the reach of his lies, whether
they are inspired by self-interest or generosity. The
diversity of languages therefore works like Necessity,
and it is because of this that it gives rise to a form of
the tragic.

So the restoration of spoken language, first invented in the playful mimicry of the picturesque,
ended by expressing the whole content of social contradiction. In Céline's work, for instance, writing is
not at the service of thought, like some successfully
realistic décor tacked on to the description of a social
sub-class; it really represents the writer's descent into
the sticky opacity of the condition which he is describing. True, this is still a way of *expressing* it, and
Literature has not been left behind. But it must be
agreed that, among all the means of *description* (since
until now Literature has above all aimed at that), the

adoption of a real language is for the writer the most human act. And a sizable part of modern Literature is pervaded by the more or less elaborate shreds of this dream: a literary language which might emulate the naturalness of social languages. (We have only to think of the dialogues in Sartre's novels to give a recent and well-known example.) But however successful these pictures may be, they can never be any more than reproductions, arias, so to speak, surrounded by long recitatives in an entirely conventional mode of writing.

Queneau has tried, precisely, to show that it was possible to contaminate all the parts of the written discourse by spoken speech, and in his works the socialization of literary language takes a simultaneous hold on all the layers of writing: the spelling, the vocabulary, and – which is more important although less spectacular – the pace. Of course, this writing of Queneau's is not situated outside Literature, since it is still consun.ed by a limited section of society; it is not the vehicle of a universality, but only of an experiment and an entertainment. At least, for the first time, it is not the writing which is literary; Literature is expelled from Form and is now nothing but a category. Here, it is Literature which is irony, and language which is experienced in depth. Or rather, Literature is openly reduced to the problematics of language; and indeed, that is all it can now be.

We can see taking shape, by this means, the possible area of a new humanism : the general suspicion which has gradually overtaken language throughout modern literature gives way to a reconciliation between the logos of the writer and that of men. Only then can the writer declare himself entirely committed, when his poetic freedom takes its place within a verbal condition whose limits are those of society and not those of a convention or a public. Otherwise, commitment will always be purely nominal; it will be able to effect the salvation of one conscience, but not to provide a basis for action. It is because there is no thought without language, that Form is the first and last arbiter of literary responsibility, and it is because there is no reconciliation within the present society, that language, necessary and necessarily orientated, creates for the writer a situation fraught with conflict.

THE UTOPIA OF LANGUAGE

The multiplication of modes of writing is a modern phenomenon which forces a choice upon the writer, making form a kind of behaviour and giving rise to an ethic of writing. To all the dimensions which together made up the literary creation is henceforth added a new depth, since form is by itself a kind of parasitical mechanism of the intellectual function. Modern writing is a truly independent organism which grows around the literary act, decorates it with a value which is foreign to its intention, ceaselessly commits it to a double mode of existence, and superimposes upon the content of the words opaque signs which carry with them a history, a second-order meaning which compromises or redeems it, so that with the situation of thought is mingled a supplementary fate, often diverging from the former and always an encumbrance to it – the fate of the form.

Now this fatal character of the literary sign, which makes a writer unable to pen a word without taking a pose characteristic of an out-of-date, anarchic or imitative language – one in any case conventionalized and dehumanized – has taken effect precisely at the moment when Literature, abolishing more and more its condition as a bourgeois myth, is required as a document or a testimony of a humanism which has at last integrated History into its image of man. So that the old literary categories, emptied in the best instances of their traditional content, which was the expression of an intemporal essence of man, eventually stand only by virtue of a specific form, an order due to the vocabulary or the syntax, in short, quite simply a language: it is now writing which absorbs the whole identity of a literary work. A novel by Sartre is a novel only to the extent of its having remained faithful to a certain recitative tone, which is, moreover, intermittent, and whose norms have been established in the course of a whole previous geology of the novel: in fact, it is the mode of writing of the recitative, and not its content, which reintegrates the Sartrean novel into the category of Belles-Lettres. Furthermore, when Sartre attempts to break the time-flow typical of the novel, and duplicates his narrative in order to render the ubiquity of reality (in *The Reprieve*), it is the narrative mode of writing which re-composes, above the simultaneity of the events, a Time which is undivided and homogeneous, the Time of the Narrator, whose particular voice, defined by highly recognizable contingent features, burdens the unfolding of History with a parasitical unity, and gives the novel the ambiguity of a testimony which may well be false.

This shows that a modern masterpiece is impossible, since the writer is forced by his writing into a cleft stick : either the object of the work is naively attuned to the conventions of its form, Literature remaining deaf to our present History, and not going beyond the literary myth; or else the writer acknowledges the vast novelty of the present world, but finds that in order to express it he has at his disposal only a language which is splendid but lifeless. In front of the virgin sheet of paper, at the moment of choosing the words which must frankly signify his place in History, and testify that he assumes its data, he observes a tragic disparity between what he does and what he sees. Before his eyes, the world of society now exists as a veritable Nature, and this Nature speaks, elaborating living languages from which the writer is excluded: on the contrary, History puts in his hands a decorative and compromising instrument, a writing inherited from a previous and different History, for which he is not responsible and yet which is the only one he can use. Thus is born a tragic element in writing, since the conscious writer must henceforth fight against ancestral and a'l-powerful signs which, from the depths of a past foreign to him, impose Literature on him like some ritual, not like a reconciliation.

Therefore, unless they renounced Literature, the solution of this problematic of writing does not depend on the writer. Every writer born opens within himself the trial of literature, but if he condemns it, he always grants it a reprieve which literature turns to use in order to reconquer him. However hard he tries to create a free language, it comes back to him fabricated, for luxury is never innocent : and it is this stale language, closed by the immense pressure of all the men who do not speak it, which he must continue to use. Writing therefore is a blind alley, and it is because society itself is a blind alley. The writers of today feel this; for them, the search for a non-style or an oral style, for a zero level or a spoken level of writing is, all things considered, the anticipation of a homogeneous social state; most of them understand that there can be no universal language outside a concrete, and no longer a mystical or merely nomi-nal, universality of society.

There is therefore in every present mode of writing a double postulation : there is the impetus of a break and the impetus of a coming to power, there is the very shape of every revolutionary situation, the fundamental ambiguity of which is that Revolution must of necessity borrow, from what it wants to destroy, the very image of what it wants to possess. Like modern art in its entirety, literary writing carries at the same time the alienation of History and the dream of History; as a Necessity, it testifies to the division of languages which is inseparable from the division of classes; as Freedom, it is the consciousness of this division and the very effort which seeks to surmount it. Feeling permanently guilty of its own solitude, it is none the less an imagination eagerly desiring a felicity of words, it hastens towards a dreamed-of language whose freshness, by a kind of ideal anticipation, might portray the perfection of some new Adamic world where language would no longer be alienated. The proliferation of modes of writing brings a new Literature into being in so far as the latter invents its language only in order to be a project: Literature becomes the Utopia of language.